Contents

GW00671684

Introduction

I cannot begin to estimate the number of times that I have waited to photograph a favourite diesel locomotive heading a train in a location that I've travelled a long way to reach. When the sun goes in or something else goes wrong, it is particularly disheartening when the photograph is a once-only opportunity in some distant land. Fortunately, with careful planning and preparation, everything often comes together and a sense of satisfaction results, as well as a photograph that I'm happy for others to view.

My interest in railways began at a very early age, with occasional visits to local railway stations with my father and other family members. But it was during a family holiday in 1959 at Dawlish, Devon, that my enthusiasm for railways really took off. I was eleven years old and, while it was mainly the Great Western steam locomotives heading their trains along the coast that caught my eye, the new British Railways diesels were also something different and exciting. Every day, I would look forward to seeing the Warship Class diesel-hydraulics D600 *Active* and D601 *Ark Royal* passing by on the Up and Down 'Cornish Riviera Express'.

Later, I remember my delight at seeing the D200 series English Electric Type 4 diesel-electrics for the first time at Rugby, working expresses on the West Coast Main Line, soon after their introduction to the London Midland region of British Railways.

My hobby gradually progressed from trainspotting to photography. My father was a keen photographer who did his own processing of black and white film. His interest passed on to me and I began taking occasional photographs, often with limited success, of my favourite locomotives and trains. At first, I used box cameras or a Kodak Brownie 127, which were not the most suitable cameras for what I was trying to do. I later progressed to 35-mm cameras and a Mamiyaflex C2 twin lens reflex taking 120 roll film. In more recent years, like most other photographers, I have moved to digital cameras with their many advantages. Most of the photographs in this book were taken with Minolta SRT101, Pentax MX, and Canon film cameras, while the later photos were taken using various Canon digital single lens reflexes.

I lost interest in railways towards the end of steam on Britain's main lines. The sight of once splendid steam engines in very dirty, run-down condition with nameplates removed was very depressing and so, for a few years, my attention was focused elsewhere.

In 1969, a visit to Wales with some friends provided a glimpse of the Talyllyn Railway and one of its trains with *Douglas* in charge. It was my first sight of a steam-operated narrow gauge railway and I was hooked. Visits to various other narrow gauge railways in England and Wales followed and I went to Europe for the first time in 1971,

DIESEL LOCOMOTIVES AROUND THE WORLD

PETER J. GREEN

AMBERLEY

Acknowledgement

My thanks are once again due to Val Brown for her assistance with checking my text for errors.

First published 2023

Amberley Publishing
The Hill, Stroud
Gloucestershire, GL5 4EP

www.amberley-books.com

Copyright © Peter J. Green, 2023

The right of Peter J. Green to be identified as
the Author of this work has been asserted in
accordance with the Copyrights, Designs and
Patents Act 1988.

ISBN 978 1 3981 0852 3 (print)
ISBN 978 1 3981 0853 0 (ebook)

British Library Cataloguing in Publication Data.
A catalogue record for this book is available from
the British Library.

Typesetting by SJmagic DESIGN SERVICES, India.
Printed in the UK.

a camping holiday in my Morris Mini-Minor, to see narrow gauge railways in France, Germany and Switzerland. However, it was the standard gauge steam in Germany, France and Northern Italy that revived my general interest in railways.

After my first overseas holiday I began to make frequent trips abroad to view and photograph railways, as well as to experience other countries. Initially, the trips were made with organisations such as the Worcester Locomotive Society, with whom I had visited many railway installations in Britain previously, and the Locomotive Club of Great Britain, as well as independently. I have always preferred the freedom of independent travel, but often it has been necessary to visit with groups for access to installations or for the use of special trains.

At first, the visits were mainly for the surviving steam operations and, while diesels were not ignored, limited film supplies meant that they were not photographed as often as I would have liked. On later visits, the opposite was often the case, and steam was very much a second priority. The diesel operations in various countries have provided some of my best railway experiences. In particular, I have enjoyed the ALCo DL500 diesels in the Bolān Pass in Pakistan, the Anglo-Franco-Belge GMs on the Athus-Meuse line in Belgium, freight trains at Cajon and Tehachapi and electro-diesels in the Hudson Valley in the USA, and the old General Electric locomotives in Thailand, as well as many other operations around the world. We all have our favourite locomotive types. For me, the products of ALCo, English Electric and General Electric appeal the most because of the noise from their engines and, particularly in the case of the ALCos, the smoke they make, but I also like the E and F units and related types produced by General Motors.

This book, in which I've tried to give a flavour of overseas railway systems, contains a selection of diesel photos taken during my travels to various countries, commencing in 1975. Unfortunately, the diesel scene in many parts of the world is now a shadow of what it was. The number of locomotive manufacturers has decreased significantly as a result of closures, mergers and takeovers, resulting in greater standardisation, although one relatively recent development is the emergence of China as a significant exporter of diesels to the countries of South East Asia and elsewhere. However, slowly spreading electrification, modern diesel railcars and quieter, less impressive diesel locomotives, while providing more efficient transport, are all playing a part in gradually making the railways less interesting for many enthusiasts. In spite of all this, there are still many countries around the world that have much to interest the visiting diesel enthusiast and photographer.

Although the railways are being modernised at varying rates, many Asian countries still have interesting diesel operations. I particularly enjoy visiting South East Asia, where I expect that the railway operations will encourage me to continue my travels for some years to come.

Peter J. Green.
Worcester, England.
2021

Australia

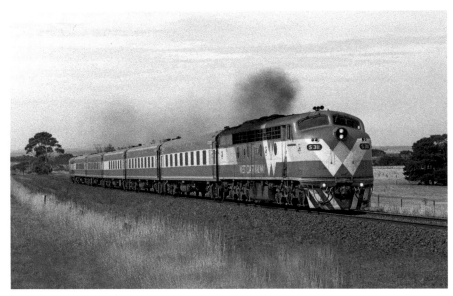

Pictured west of Geelong, West Coast Railway S311, based on the General Motors Electro-Motive Division (EMD) F7 type and built by Clyde Engineering, heads the 12.35 Melbourne Spencer Street to Warrnambool service. Eighteen S Class locomotives were built between 1957 and 1961, with this example entering service in November 1960. 28 March 2000.

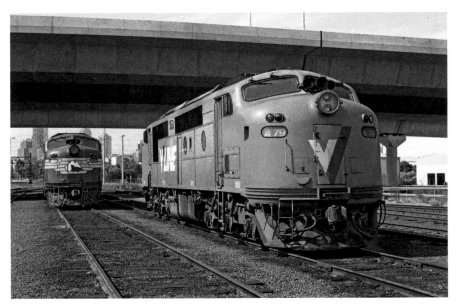

V/Line Co-Co diesel-electric A79 at South Dynon locomotive depot, Melbourne. Freight Australia A81 is on the left. The A Class are rebuilt Victorian Railways B Class locomotives, built by Clyde Engineering in 1952 and 1953 and rebuilt in the 1980s. 4 April 2000.

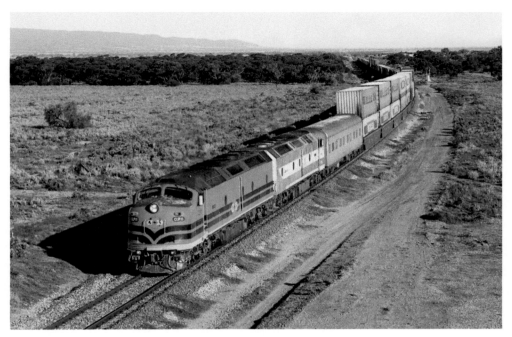

Co-Co diesel-electric CLP11 *Kaurna* leads a second CL on a double-stack container train, bound for Perth, at Port Germein, South Australia. The CL Class of seventeen locomotives was built by Clyde Engineering for the Commonwealth Railways between 1970 and 1972. The locomotives were rebuilt by Morrison Knudsen in the 1990s, seven as CLFs for freight service and ten as CLPs with head end power for passenger duties. 29 March 2000.

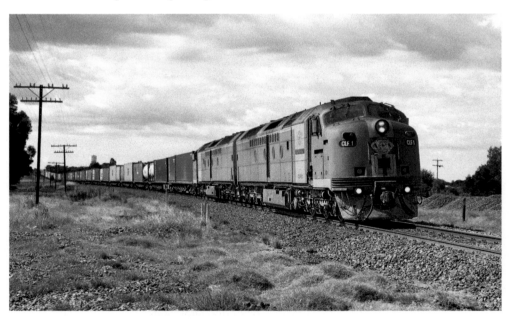

Clyde Engineering Co-Co diesel-electric CLF1 *City of Whyalla* and a second CL, both rebuilt by Morrison Knudsen, head a northbound container train into Nhill, Victoria. 2 April 2000.

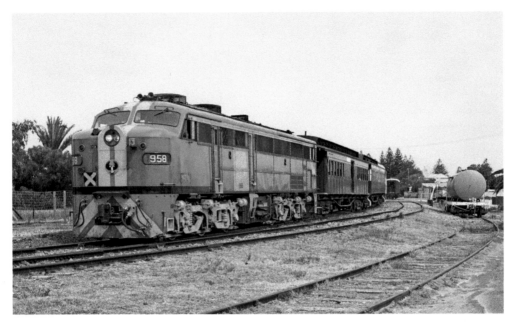

ALCo 930 Class Co-Co diesel-electric No. 958 shunts its train at Victor Harbor after arriving from Mount Barker on the SteamRanger Heritage Railway in South Australia. Thirty-seven of these locomotives, model DL500B, were built by AE Goodwin between 1955 and 1967. 22 October 2000.

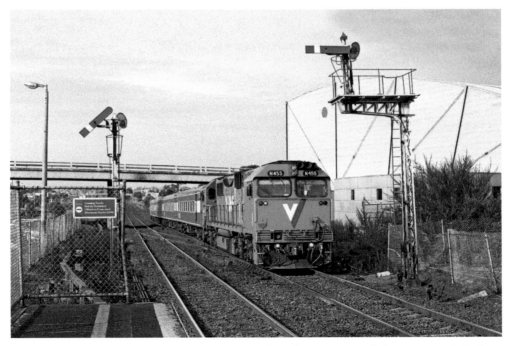

V/Line Co-Co diesel-electric N455 approaches North Geelong station with the 08.30 South Geelong to Melbourne Spencer Street, Victoria. Note the somersault signal. Twenty-five N Class locomotives, EMD model JT22HC-2, were built by Clyde Engineering between 1985 and 1987. 27 March 2000.

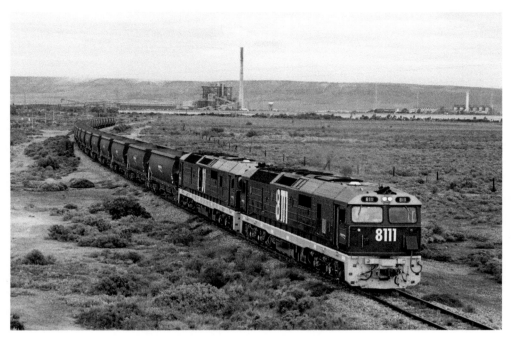

New South Wales 81 Class Co-Co diesel-electrics Nos 8111 and 8101 head an empty coal train to Leigh Creek away from Playford power station, Port Augusta, South Australia. Eighty-four 81 Class locomotives, EMD model JT26C-2SS, were built by Clyde Engineering between 1982 and 1991. 30 March 2000.

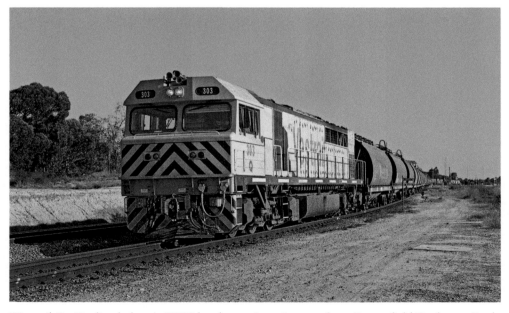

Westrail Co-Co diesel-electric Q303 heads a grain train away from Forrestfield Yard, near Perth, Western Australia. Nineteen of these locomotives, EMD model GT46C, were built for Westrail by Clyde Engineering at Forrestfield in 1997 and 1998. 27 October 2000.

Austria

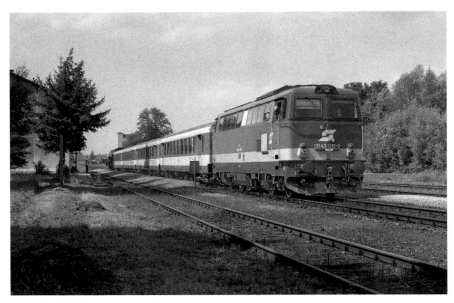

Österreichische Bundesbahnen B-B diesel-hydraulic No. 2043 012 waits to depart from Grafenstein with the 13.04 Klagenfurt to Zeltweg. Seventy-seven of these locomotives, fitted with Jenbach LM1500 engines, were built by Jenbacher Werke AG between 1964 and 1977. 28 August 1997.

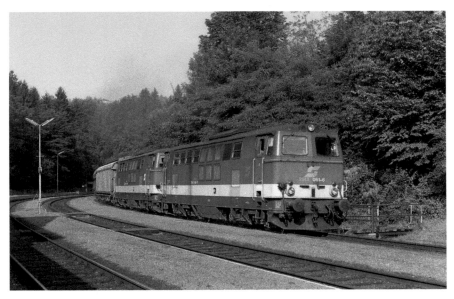

Österreichische Bundesbahnen B-B diesel-hydraulics Nos 2143 061 and 2143 068 head an eastbound freight through Lassnitzhöhe. Seventy-seven of these locomotives, fitted with SGP T12c engines, were built by Simmering-Graz-Pauker AG between 1964 and 1977. 25 August 1997.

Baltic States

Estonia

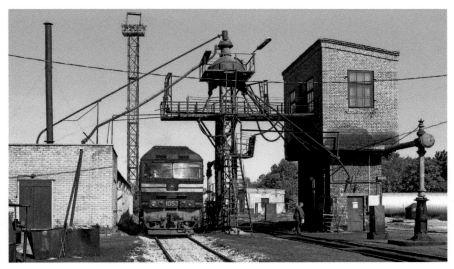

Eesti Raudtee Co-Co diesel-electric TEP70 No. 1053 (previously TEP70 No. 0329), built at the Kolomna locomotive works (Kolomensky Zavod), stands at Tallinn locomotive depot. The TEP70, introduced in 1973, is a 3,975-hp passenger locomotive. 13 June 1999.

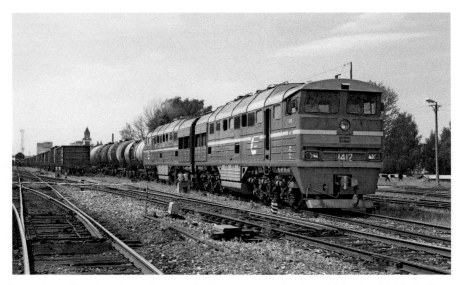

Eesti Raudtee Co-Co diesel-electric double locomotive 2TE116 No. 1412, built at the Voroshilovgrad locomotive works, Lugansk, heads a freight train out of Valga yard, Estonia. Introduced in 1971, the 2TE116 is a heavy freight locomotive used throughout the former Soviet Union. 11 June 1999.

Latvia

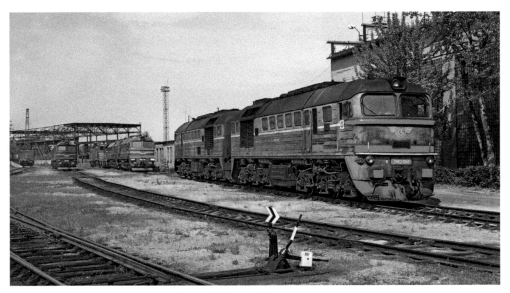

Diesel-electric double locomotive 2M62 No. 0519, built at Lugansk, is pictured at Daugavpils locomotive depot, Latvia. Two similar locomotives are in the background. The Co-Co M62 was a heavy freight locomotive, built in large numbers and used in the Soviet Union and many Eastern Bloc countries, as well as Cuba, North Korea and Mongolia. Double, 2M62, and triple, 3M62, versions were also built. 10 June 1999.

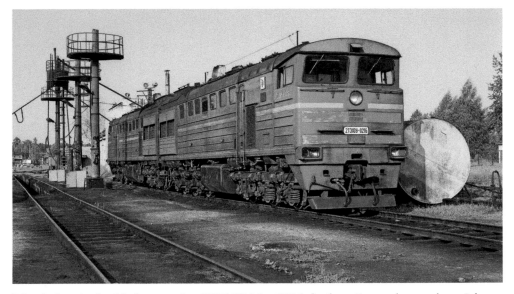

Diesel-electric double locomotive 2TE10U No. 0216, built at Lugansk, stands at Jelgava locomotive depot, Latvia. The Co-Co TE10, introduced in 1958, was a more powerful version of the TE3. Two-, three- and four-unit locomotives were also constructed. The 2TE10U was an advanced version of the 2TE10. 8 June 1999.

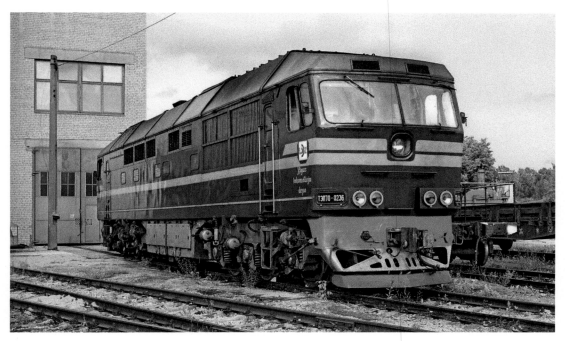

Co-Co diesel-electric TEP70 No. 0236, built for use on passenger trains, stands at Riga Zasulaks locomotive depot, Latvia. 9 June 1999.

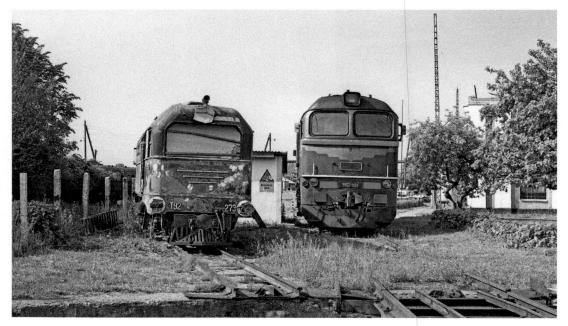

Withdrawn 750-mm gauge TU2 Bo-Bo diesel-electric No. 273 and 1,520-mm gauge M62 Co-Co diesel-electric No. 1151 stand next to the mixed gauge turntable at Gulbene locomotive depot, Latvia. Introduced in 1955, 281 TU2 locomotives were built at the Kaluga machine factory. 11 June 1999.

Lithuania

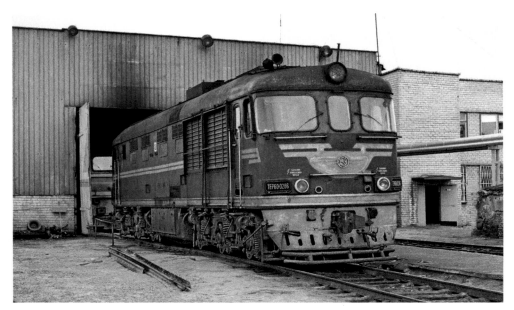

Co-Co diesel-electric locomotive TEP60 No. 0286 stands at Vilnius LT1 diesel depot, Lithuania. The TEP60 is a passenger locomotive introduced in 1960. The Kolomna factory built 1,472 single units and 116 double locomotives between 1960 and 1985. 5 June 1999.

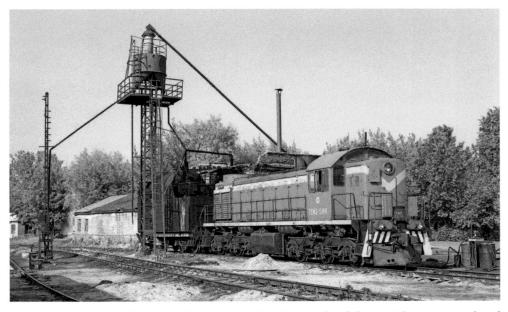

Co-Co diesel-electric TEM2 No. 5114 is pictured at Kaunas diesel depot, Lithuania. Introduced in 1960, TEM2 class locomotives were built at both the Bryansk engineering plant and the Voroshilovgrad diesel locomotive plant in the USSR. The design is based on the American ALCo RSD1. 6 June 1999.

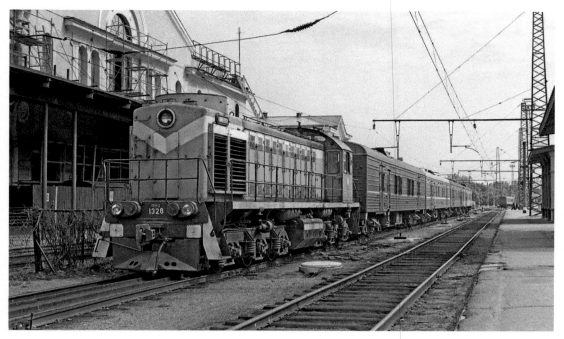

Running long hood forward, Co-Co diesel-electric TEM2 No. 1328 heads a passenger train at Vilnius, Lithuania. 5 June 1999.

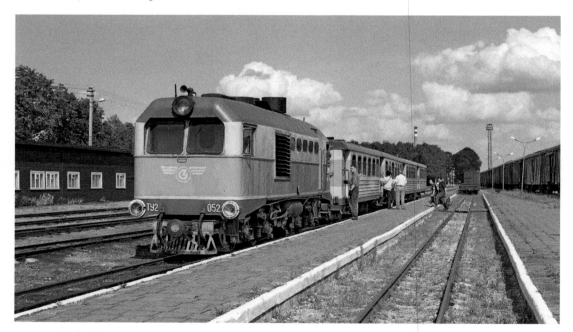

With the locomotive and coaches in matching livery, 750-mm gauge Bo-Bo diesel-electric TU2 No. 052, built at Kaluga, stands at Panevėžys station, Lithuania, with the 16.00 Panevėžys to Anykščiai. In 1996, the railway was given protected status as an item of cultural heritage importance. 5 June 1999.

Belarus

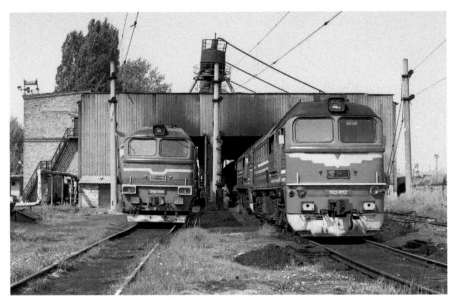

Double and single versions of the M62 Co-Co diesel-electric locomotive stand at Brest East locomotive depot, Belarus. Double locomotive 2M62 No. 0881 is on the left, and M62 No. 1052 is on the right. 8 June 1998.

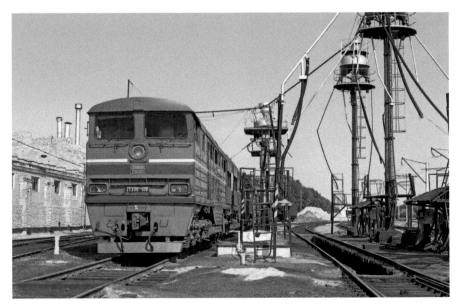

Co-Co diesel-electric double locomotive 2TE116 No. 618, built at Lugansk, is pictured at Grebenka locomotive depot, Belarus. 10 June 1998.

Belgium

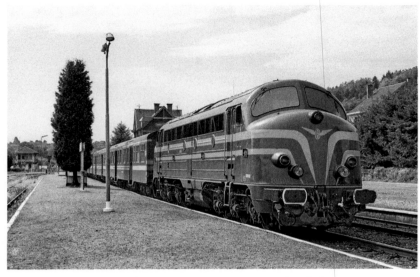

Société Nationale des Chemins de Fer Belges (SNCB) Co-Co diesel-electric No. 204.004 stands at Houyet after arriving with the 10.46 Dinant to Houyet. This is an un-rebuilt example of the General Motors locomotives built under licence by Nydqvist and Holm AB (NOHAB) and Société Anglo-Franco-Belge (AFB). This locomotive was built by AFB in 1957 and is a Belgian museum locomotive. 28 May 1995.

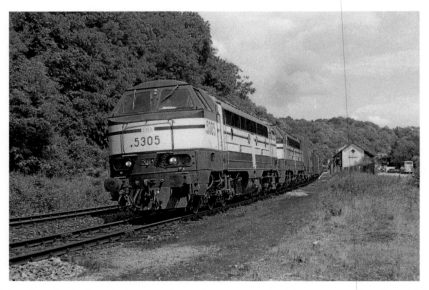

SNCB Co-Co diesel-electric locomotives Nos 5305 and 5307, previously Class 203, head a southbound freight along the Athus-Meuse line, through Anseremme, Belgium. These locomotives, rebuilt with floating cabs, were built by AFB in 1955 under licence from General Motors, for use on heavy freight trains. 27 May 1995.

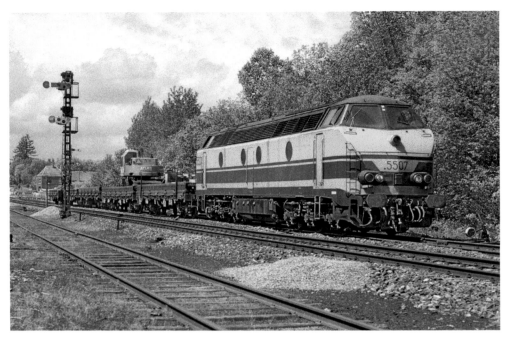

SNCB Co-Co diesel-electric No. 5507 is pictured on permanent way duty at Graide, Belgium. Forty-two of these diesel-electric locomotives, powered by GM 16-567 C engines, were built by La Brugeoise et Nivelles of Belgium in 1961 and 1962. 29 May 1995.

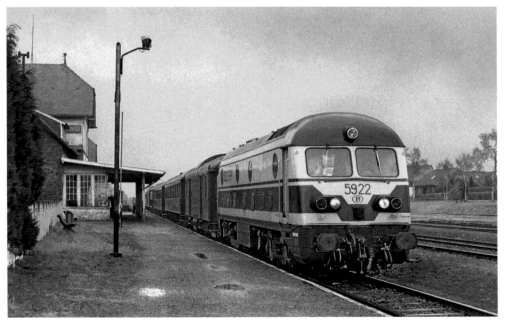

Bo-Bo diesel-electric No. 5922 waits at Sourbrodt, Belgium, with the 10.00 Vennbahn service from Eupen to Bütgenbach. Originally SNCB Class 201, fifty-five of these locomotives were assembled at the John Cockerill factories in Seraing in 1954. The Vennbahn is now closed. 27 May 1996.

Bosnia

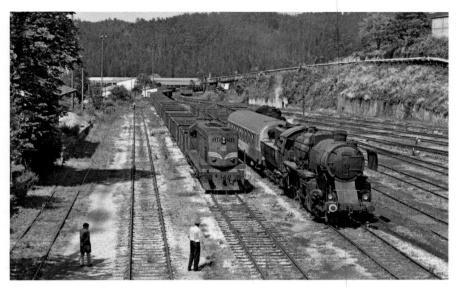

Željeznice Federacije Bosne i Hercegovine (ŽFBH) No. 661.30, a General Motors model G16 diesel-electric, arrives at Banovići Oskovo separacija with a train of empty coal wagons. On the right, 2-10-0 steam locomotive No. 33.248 stands at the head of a Railway Touring Company special train, with a second steam locomotive, No. 19.12, behind. 12 June 2019.

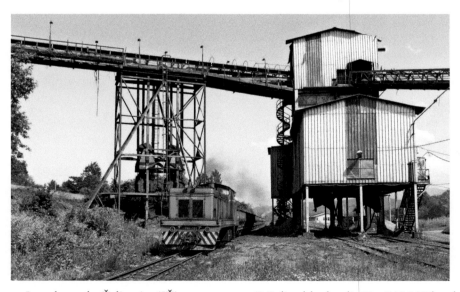

Former Jugoslovenske Željeznice (JŽ) narrow gauge B-B diesel-hydraulic No. 740.107 heads an empty coal train from Banovići, bound for Turija opencast mine, past the loader at Grivice. Forty of these 760-mm gauge locomotives were built for JŽ by Đuro Đaković at Slavonski Brod, under licence from SACM, between 1968 and 1971. Four of these were later purchased to operate the coal traffic associated with the mines around Banovići. 13 June 2019.

Cambodia

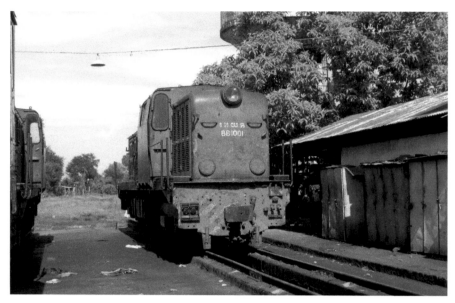

Alsthom Bo-Bo diesel-electric BB1001 stands at Phnom Penh locomotive depot. This is one of six single cab locomotives supplied to Cambodia in 1968 and 1969. It is model AD12B (single cab) and is fitted with a 1,200-hp engine. 11 April 2006.

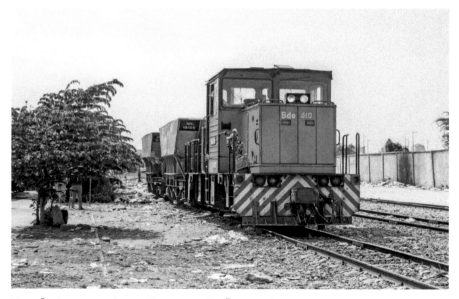

In 1994, Českomoravská-Kolben-Daněk (ČKD) of Prague supplied two 415-hp 0-4-0 diesel-electric shunting locomotives to Cambodia, model T234, Nos Bde.410 and Bde.411. Here, Bde.410 shunts ballast wagons between Phnom Penh station and the locomotive depot. 11 March 2018.

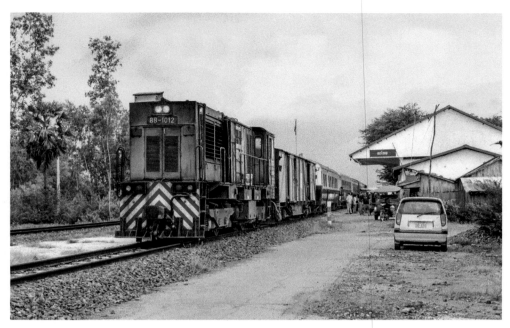

Bo-Bo diesel-electric BB.1012 pauses at Takeo, the first stop on the southern line for trains from Phnom Penh, with the 07.00 Phnom Penh to Sihanoukville. The train is formed of four diesel units, serving as coaches, and a van for motorbikes. Three of these 987-hp locomotives, model DEV-736, were built for Cambodia by ČKD in 1993. 3 March 2018.

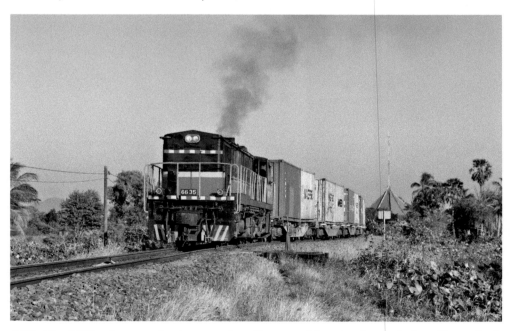

ALCo No. 6635 makes a smoky departure from Kampot with a container train from Phnom Penh to Sihanoukville. The locomotive is a former Indian Railways YDM4 diesel-electric that previously worked in Malaysia. Ten of these locomotives arrived in Cambodia in 2019. 9 December 2019.

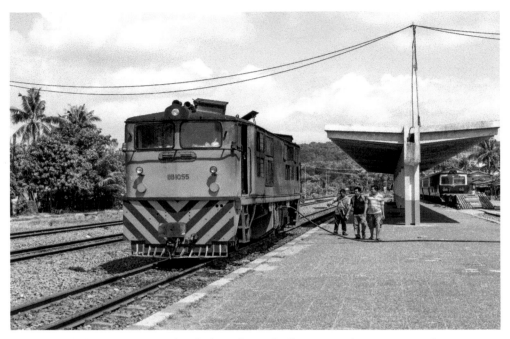

Bo-Bo diesel-electric BB1055 takes fuel at Sihanoukville station after arriving with a passenger train from Phnom Penh. The locomotive, model AD12B (double cab), is one of six 1,200-hp locomotives supplied by Alsthom in 1969. 4 March 2018.

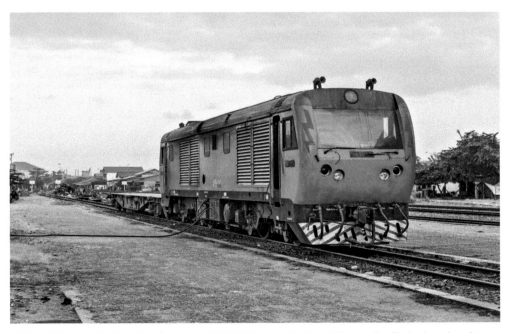

CSR Qishuyan Bo-Bo diesel-electric BB1060 takes fuel at Sihanoukville before heading a container train to Phnom Penh. One of two locomotives supplied by Qishuyan of China in 2004, it is model CKD6B fitted with a Caterpillar 3508B engine of 1,100 hp. 4 March 2018.

Canada

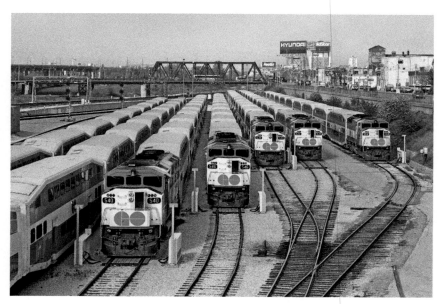

In between commuter train duties, GO Transit F59PH Bo-Bo diesel-electric locomotives are stabled with their trains at North Bathurst yard, Toronto, Canada. The locomotives are, from left to right, Nos 540, 546, 539, 534 and 559. General Motors Electro-Motive Division (EMD) built seventy-three of these 3,000-hp F59PH locomotives between 1988 and 1994. 24 May 1994.

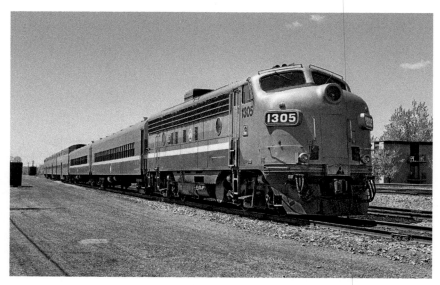

Montreal Urban Community Transit Corporation FP7A Bo-Bo diesel-electric No. 1305, built by General Motors Electro-Motive Division in 1952, is pictured stabled with its train at Dorion prior to working a local service to Windsor station, Montreal. General Motors Electro-Motive Division and General Motors Diesel (GMD, Canada) built 381 FP7s between 1949 and 1953. 29 May 1994.

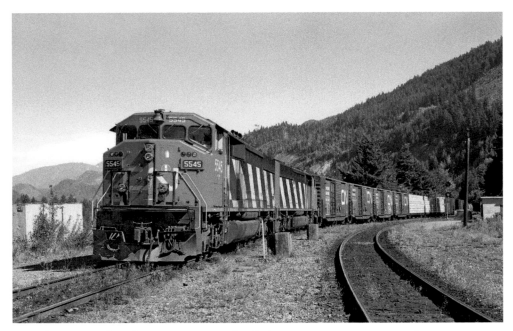

Canadian National Railway (CN) Co-Co diesel-electrics SD60F No. 5545 and SD60 No. 5455 head a southbound freight into Boston Bar, British Columbia, Canada. EMD and GMD built 1,144 3,800-hp SD60s between 1984 and 1995. 20 August 1995.

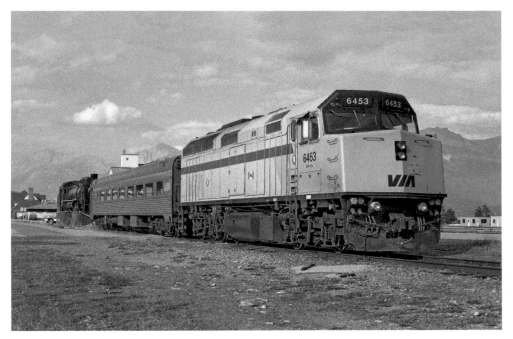

Via Rail Bo-Bo diesel-electric F40PH-2D No. 6453, built by GMD at London, Ontario, in 1989, is pictured at Jasper, British Columbia. Fifty-nine of these locomotives were built for Via Rail between 1986 and 1989. CN No. 6015 4-8-2 Class U-1-a steam locomotive is behind. 22 August 1995.

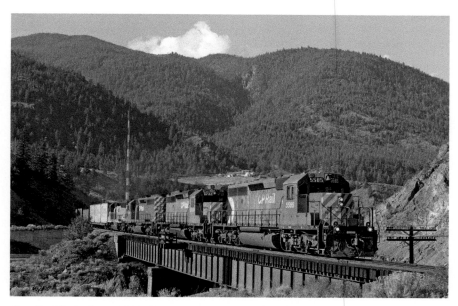

Canadian Pacific Railway (CP) GMD SD40-2 Co-Co diesel-electrics Nos 5585, 5733, 5745 and an unidentified locomotive are pictured on a freight working in the Thompson River canyon between Spences Bridge and Lytton, British Columbia. The 3,000-hp SD40-2 road switcher is a development of the successful SD40. More than 4,000 were built between 1972 and 1989. 30 August 1995.

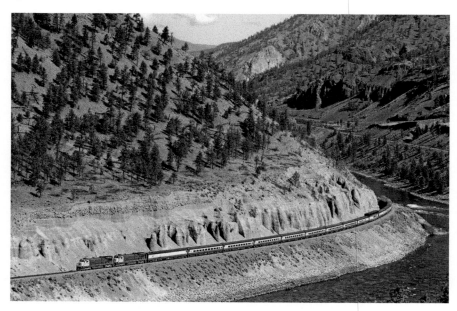

Former Atchison, Topeka & Santa Fe Railway B36-7 Bo-Bo diesel-electrics Nos 7498 and 7488 head the Rocky Mountaineer tourist train from Jasper and Banff to Vancouver through the Thompson River canyon between Spences Bridge and Lytton, British Columbia, Canada. Between 1980 and 1985, 222 of these 3,600-hp locomotives were built by General Electric Transportation Systems (GE). 30 August 1995.

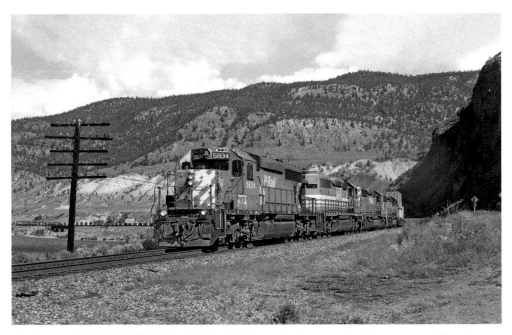

Work-worn CP Rail SD40-2 No. 5834 leads three other locomotives in a variety of liveries on a westbound container train, alongside the Thompson River, near Spences Bridge. 30 August 1995.

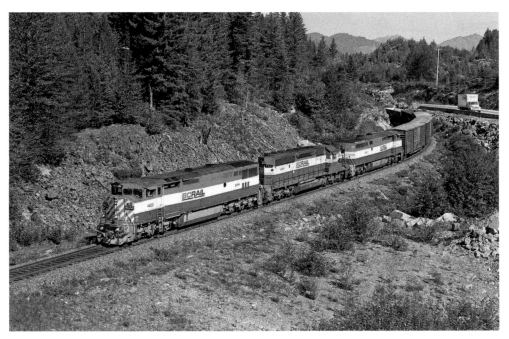

BCRail Co-Co diesel-electrics GE Dash 8-40CM No. 4622, EMD SD40-2 No. 743 and GE Dash 8-40CM No. 4614 head a southbound mixed freight south of Whistler, British Columbia, Canada. Introduced in 1990, GE supplied twenty-six 4,000-hp Dash 8-40CM locomotives to BCRail. 1 September 1995.

China

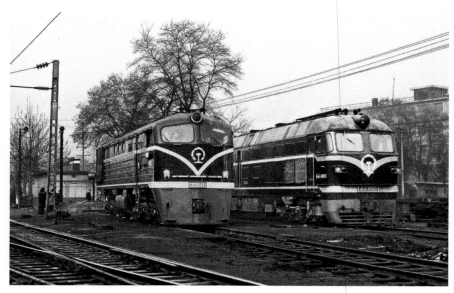

DF Class No. 1219 and DF4 Class No. 6065 Co-Co diesel-electrics stand in the gloom at Lanzhou locomotive depot, China. The single-ended DF class was China's first production main line diesel locomotive. Introduced in 1964 and fitted with an 1,800-hp engine, it was derived from the Soviet TE3. Around 700 DFs were built. 17 January 1992.

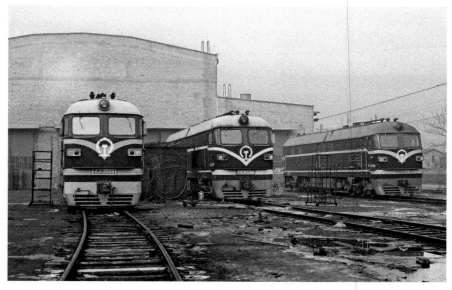

DF4 Co-Co diesel-electrics Nos 6069, 3257 and 6139 stand at Lanzhou locomotive depot, China. Introduced in 1969, the DF4, powered by a 3,250-hp V16 engine, was China's standard main line diesel locomotive, produced in very large numbers by Dalian, Qishuyan, Sifang and Datong. 17 January 1992.

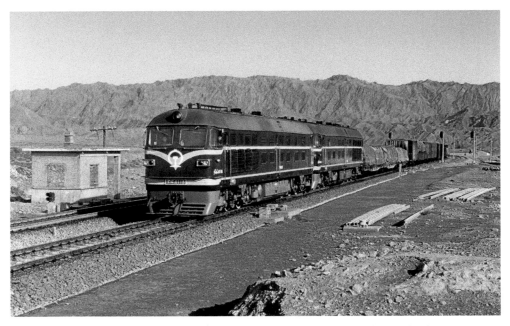

The photographer attracts the attention of the crew as a pair of Chinese-built DF4 Co-Co diesel-electrics, with No. 6118 leading, head an eastbound mixed freight train at Pingkouxia, west of Hexipu, on the main line from Lanzhou to Wulumuqi. 15 January 1992.

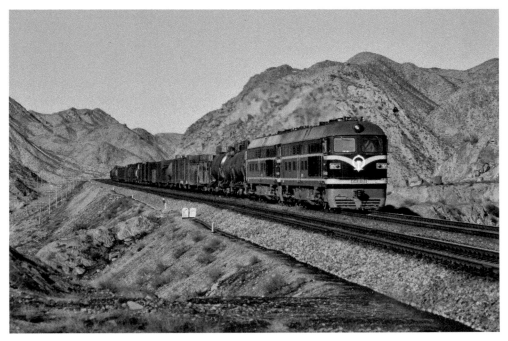

DF4B No. 6124, built by Datong, leads a second DF4 on an eastbound freight near Pingkouxia, China. At this time, the DF4s were beginning to replace the QJ 2-10-2 steam locomotives on the line. 14 January 1992.

Croatia

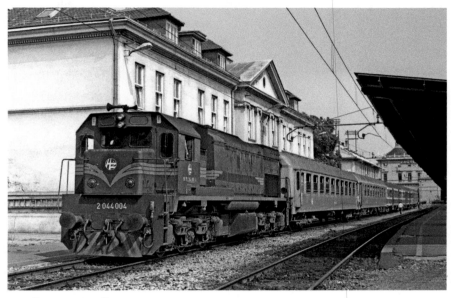

Hrvatske Željeznice (HŽ) EMD GT22HW-2 A1A-A1A diesel-electric locomotive No. 2044 004 waits for departure time at Zagreb, Croatia, with the 14.20 train from Zagreb to Čakovec. Built for JŽ between 1981 and 1984, HŽ acquired fifteen of these 2,330-hp locomotives after the breakup of Yugoslavia. 27 August 1997.

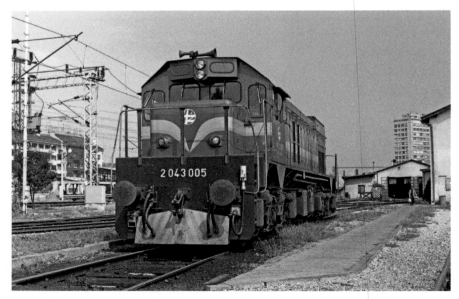

HŽ EMD A1A-A1A diesel-electric locomotive No. 2043 005, rebuilt from a 2061 Class locomotive for use on secondary lines, is pictured at Zagreb. Power output was around 1,900 hp. 27 August 1997.

Cuba

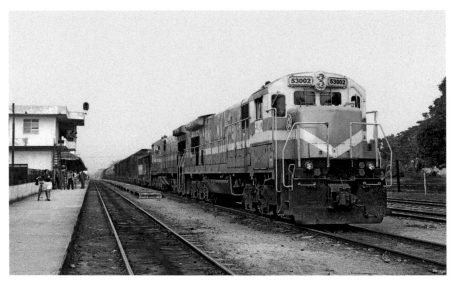

Co-Co diesel-electrics Nos 53002 and 53012 stand at the head of a mixed freight at Las Tunas station. The locomotives, both GE model C30-7, were purchased second-hand from Mexico. These successful 3,000-hp locomotives were a development of the GE U30C. More than 1,100 were built between 1976 and 1986. 14 February 2002.

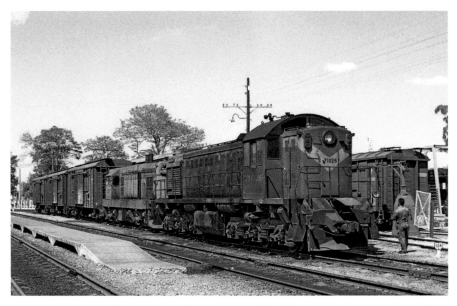

Ferrocarriles de Cuba (FCC) Co-Co diesel-electric TEM2K No. 71026 and General Motors G8 Bo-Bo diesel-electric No. 50907 shunt wagons at Bayamo. The TEM2K is a development of the Soviet TEM2, built at the Bryansk engineering works, and the GM G8 is an 875-hp locomotive built by EMD. The G8 locomotives were built between 1954 and 1965. 13 February 2002.

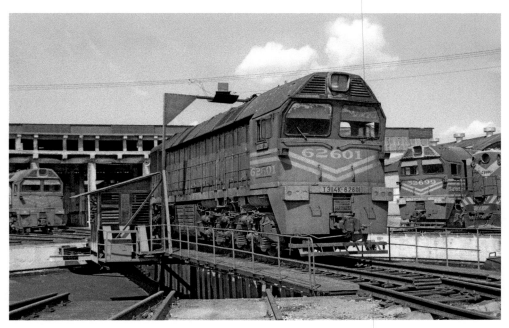

FCC 2,600 hp Co-Co diesel-electric TE114K No. 62601 runs on to the turntable at Camaguey Works, Cuba. TEM2K No. 71006 and TE114K locomotives Nos 52803 and 52699 are in the background. The TE114K locomotives were built at the Voroshilovgrad (Lugansk) diesel locomotive plant and the TEM2K at the Bryansk engineering works, USSR. 14 February 2002.

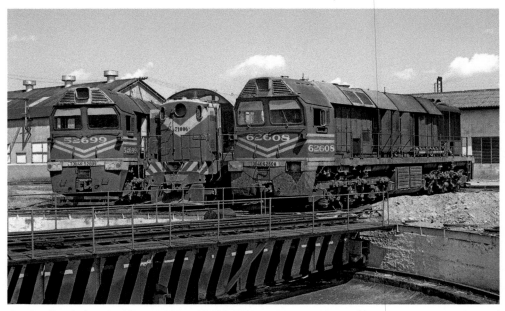

Co-Co diesel-electrics TE114K No. 52699, TEM2K No. 71006 and TE114K No. 62608 stand next to the turntable at Camaguey Works, Cuba. Designed for operation at temperatures between -15 and +50 ° C, 108 TE114K Class locomotives were delivered to Cuba between 1978 and 1984. 14 February 2002.

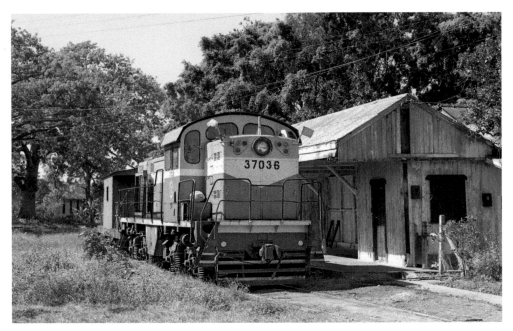

TGM4 B-B diesel-hydraulic No. 37036 is pictured at Osvaldo Sánchez sugar mill, Cuba. More than 6,500 of these 750-hp locomotives were built by the Lyudinovsky diesel locomotive plant, USSR, between 1971 and 1989. 4 February 2002.

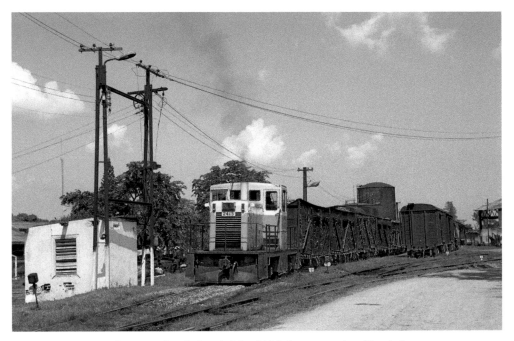

GE 30-ton centre-cab Bo-Bo diesel-electric No. 2415 shunts a train of loaded sugar cane wagons at Arquimedes Colina sugar mill, Cuba. The locomotive was purchased second-hand from the Lihue Plantation in Hawaii *c.* 1959–60. 13 February 2002.

Czech Republic

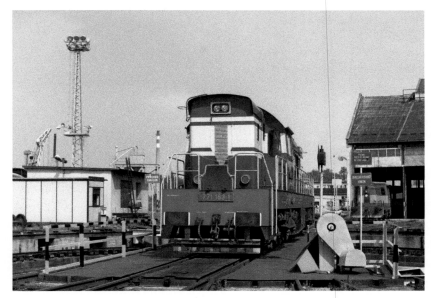

České Dráhy (ČD) Co-Co diesel-electric No. 771 183 is pictured on the turntable at Veseli nad Moravou locomotive depot. These locomotives, previously Class T669, were built by ČKD. Similar locomotives, Class ChME3, were used in large numbers in the former Soviet Union and various other countries. Approximately 8,200 were built between 1963 and 1994. 31 August 1994.

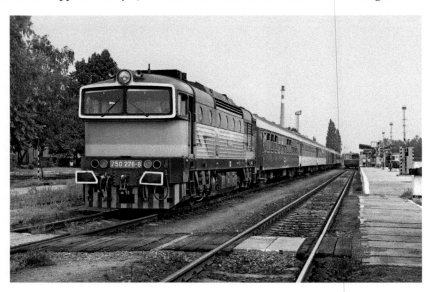

ČD Bo-Bo diesel-electric No. 750 276, a Class 753 locomotive rebuilt with electric train heating, waits at Veseli nad Moravou with the 12.49 Veseli nad Moravou to Brno. Between 1968 and 1977, 408 Class 753 locomotives were built, of which 165 were later fitted with electric train heating. 31 August 1994.

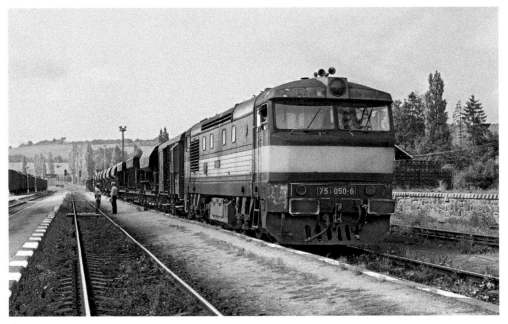

ČD Bo-Bo diesel-electric No. 751 050 shunts a freight at Okříšky after arriving from Brno. Class 751 locomotives were originally Class T478.1, built by ČKD and introduced in 1964. They are fitted with ČKD K 6 S 310 DR six-cylinder diesel engines producing around 1,500 hp. 1 September 1994.

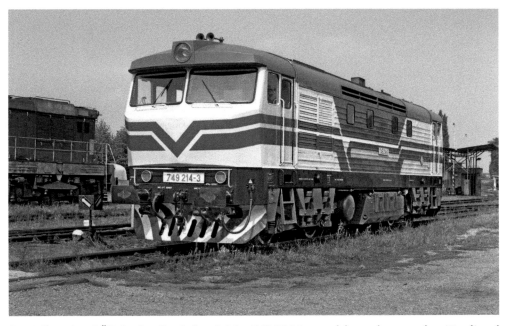

Specially painted ČD Bo-Bo diesel-electric No. 749 214 is posed for a photograph at Veseli nad Moravou locomotive depot, Czech Republic. The Class 749 was a modernised version of the Class 751 with electric train heating. 31 August 1994.

Denmark

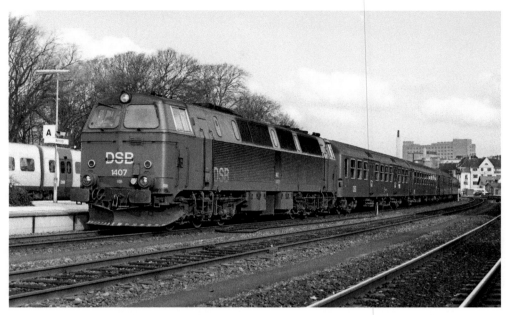

Danske Statsbaner (DSB) MZ Co-Co diesel-electric No. 1407 waits at Aalborg, Denmark, with the 10.10 Aalborg to København. This locomotive was one of the first batch of ten of this class, built between 1967 and 1969 by Nydqvist & Holm AB (NOHAB). It was fitted with an EMD 645E3 V16 engine producing 3,253 hp. 29 March 1993.

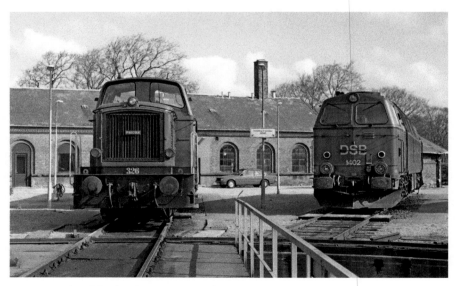

DSB MH 0-6-0 diesel-hydraulic No. 326 and MZ Co-Co diesel-electric No. 1402 stand next to the turntable at Esbjerg locomotive depot. A total of 120 440-hp Class MH locomotives were built by Frichs for DSB between 1960 and 1965. 30 March 1993.

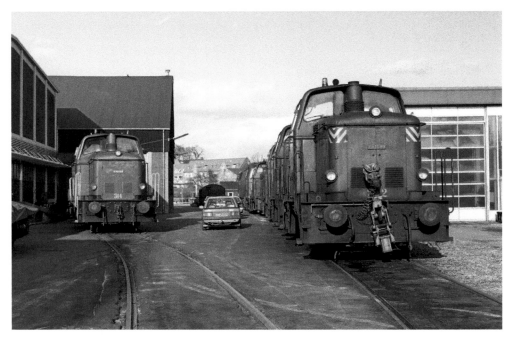

DSB MH 0-6-0 diesel-hydraulic shunter No. 314, left, stands at Aarhus locomotive depot. On the right, an unidentified MH shunter stands at the front of a line of similar locomotives with an MZ diesel-electric at the back. 28 March 1993.

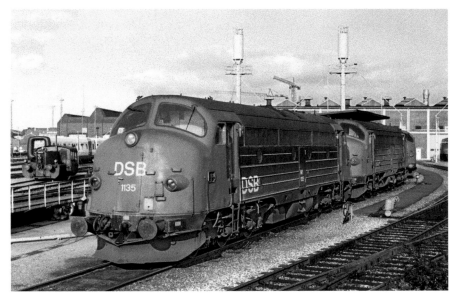

DSB NOHAB-GM MY No. 1135 of 1957 stands at the front of a line of MY A1A-A1A diesel-electric locomotives at Aarhus locomotive depot, Denmark. A Frichs Traktor is behind. Between 1954 and 1965, fifty-nine Class MY locomotives were built by Nydqvist & Holm AB under licence from General Motors. All were fitted with EMD 567 engines with power outputs of 1,700 or 1,950 hp. 28 March 1993.

France

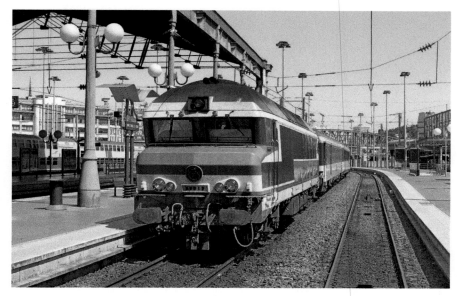

Société Nationale des Chemins de Fer Français (SNCF) Co-Co diesel-electric No. 72012 arrives at Paris Gare du Nord with the 09.21 from Laon. Ninety-two Class 72000 locomotives were built by Alsthom at Belfort between 1967 and 1974. They were fitted with Société Alsacienne de Constructions Mécaniques (SACM) AGO V16 ESHR engines producing 3,550 hp. 23 May 1998.

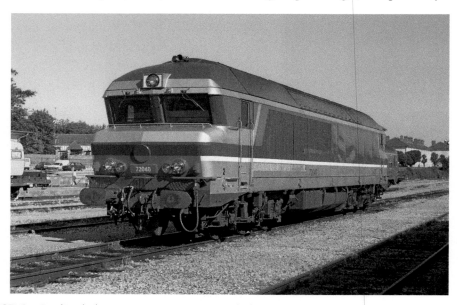

SNCF Co-Co diesel-electric No. 72040, in Corail Plus livery, stands at Troyes. This locomotive was one of thirty Class 72000 locomotives rebuilt with quieter and more efficient SEMT Pielstick engines between 2002 and 2004. 26 May 1997.

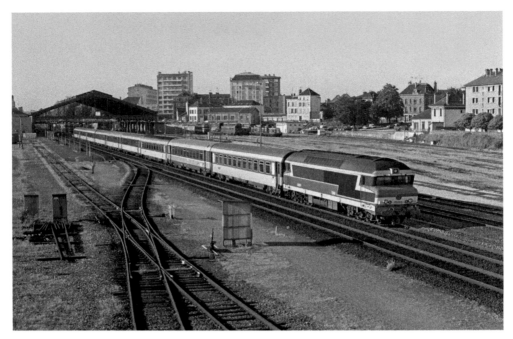

SNCF Co-Co diesel-electric No. 72066 departs from Troyes with the 05.10 Mulhouse to Paris Gare de l'Est. 26 May 1997.

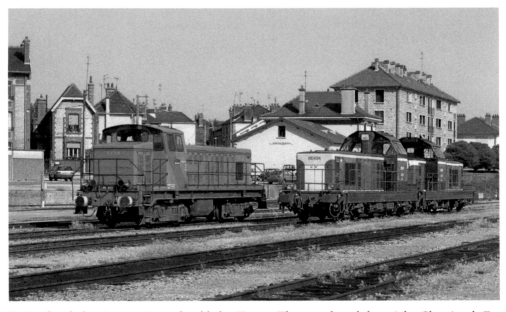

Bo-Bo diesel-electrics are pictured stabled at Troyes. They are, from left to right, Chemins de Fer et Transport Automobile (CFTA) BB4803, built by Brissonneau and Lotz, and SNCF Nos 66494 and 66431. The 1,100-hp Class 66400 locomotives were built between 1968 and 1971 by Compagnie des Ateliers et Forges de la Loire, Compagnie Electro-Méchanique, Alsthom, Fives-Lille and SACM. 25 May 1997.

Germany

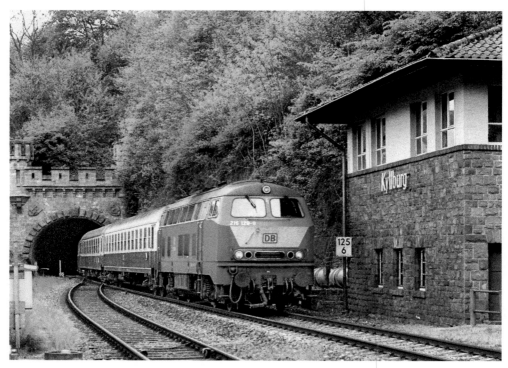

Deutsche Bahn B-B diesel-hydraulic No. 215 129 exits the tunnel at Kyllburg with the 09.49 Trier to Köln Deutz. Between 1968 and 1971, 150 Class 215 locomotives were built for the Deutsche Bundesbahn by Henschel, Krupp, Krauss-Maffei and Maschinenbau Kiel GmbH (MaK). 26 May 1996.

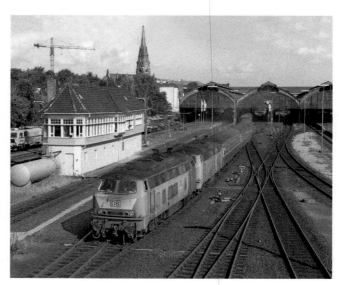

Deutsche Bahn B-B diesel-hydraulic No. 218 331 leads No. 218 337 away from Lübeck Hauptbahnhof with the 13.03 Lübeck to Hamburg. Over 400 Class 218 locomotives were built between 1968 and 1979 for the Deutsche Bundesbahn by Henschel, Krupp, Krauss-Maffei and MaK. 2 October 1995.

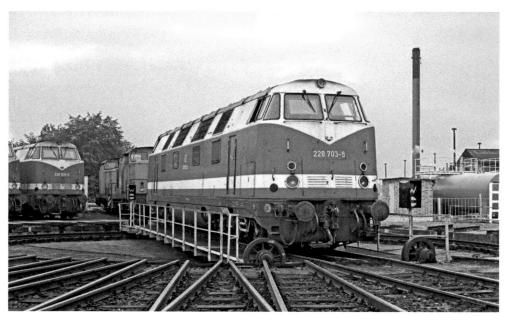

Deutsche Bahn C-C diesel-hydraulic No. 228 703 is pictured on the turntable at Brandenburg locomotive depot. The Class 228.6 was built by Lokomotivbau Karl Marx as the Class 118.2 between 1966 and 1970. The locomotives were rebuilt from 1981 by the Deutsche Reichsbahn Chemnitz Works. 9 October 1994.

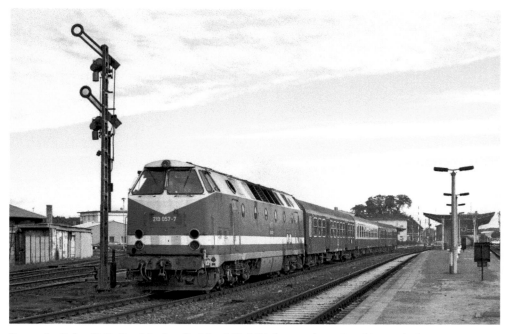

Deutsche Bahn C-C diesel-hydraulic No. 219 057 departs from Parchim with the 09.10 Waren to Ludwigslust. Between 1976 and 1985, 200 of these locomotives were built by the 23 August Locomotive Works at Bucharest for the Deutsche Reichsbahn (DR). 1 October 1995.

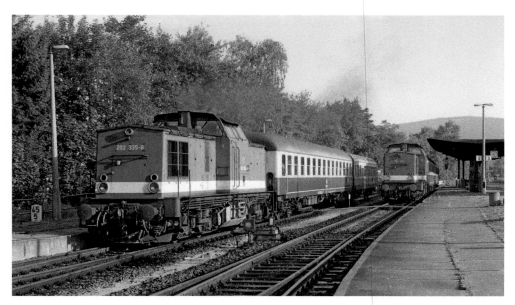

Deutsche Bahn Class 202.2 B-B diesel-hydraulics are pictured at Zella-Mehlis. On the left, No. 202 335 is departing with the 08.26 Zella-Mehlis to Wernhausen while No. 202 291 waits with the 08.58 to Meinigen. Between 1964 and 1983, around 1,000 Class 202 locomotives were built by Lokomotivbau-Elektrotechnische Werke (LEW), Hennigsdorf, as DR Class V 100. The locomotives were rebuilt from 1981 by the DR Stendal Works. 26 August 1996.

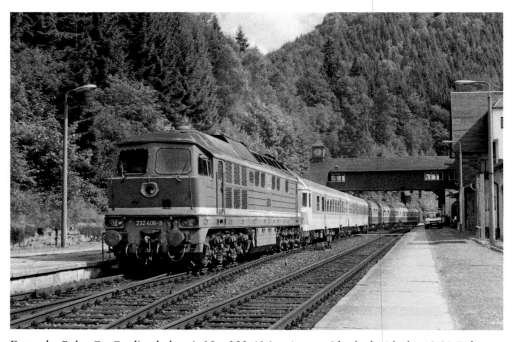

Deutsche Bahn Co-Co diesel-electric No. 232 406 arrives at Oberhof with the 10.32 Erfurt to Meiningen. The Class 232 is the former DR 'Ludmilla' Class 132. Over 700 of these 3,000-hp locomotives were built at Lugansk between 1973 and 1982. 26 August 1996.

Greece

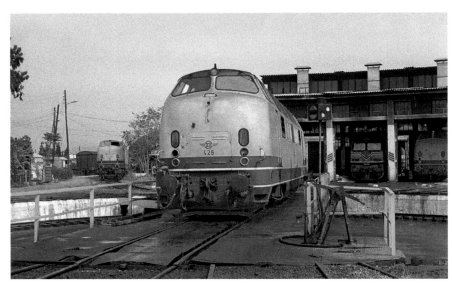

Former DB V200.1 B-B diesel-hydraulic A.426 runs on to the turntable at Athens St John's standard gauge locomotive depot. A second member of the class, A.418, is on the left and A.554 and A.414 are inside the shed. Between 1962 and 1965, fifty of these twin-engined, 2,700-hp locomotives, a more powerful version of the V200, were built for DB by Krauss-Maffei. After withdrawal by DB in 1988, twenty V200.1 locomotives were sold to Greece. 7 October 1992.

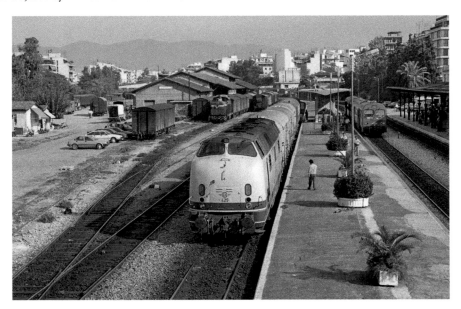

Hellenic Railways Organisation (OSE) Krauss-Maffei V200.1 B-B diesel-hydraulic A.425 arrives at Athens with a freight from the north. B-B diesel-hydraulic shunter A.156, built by the 23 August Locomotive Works at Bucharest, is on the left. 8 October 1992.

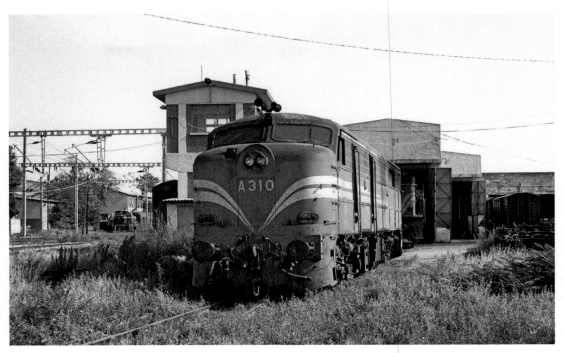

OSE 1,800-hp Co-Co diesel-electric A.310 stands at Thessaloniki locomotive depot. This is an ALCo 'World Series' export locomotive, model DL500C, built in 1963. ALCo DL543 hood unit A.321 is inside the shed and a Krupp diesel-hydraulic shunter is on the left. 10 October 1992.

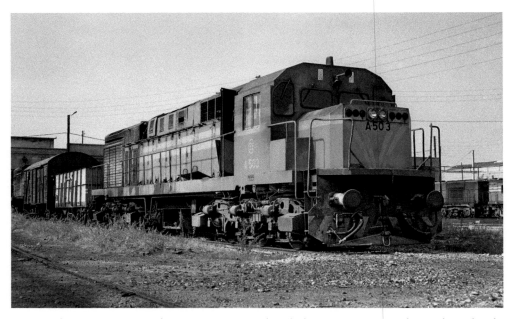

Montreal Locomotive Works (MLW) Co-Co diesel-electric A.503 stands at Thessaloniki locomotive depot. Fitted with electric train heating, ten of these 3,600-hp locomotives, model MX-636, were supplied to OSE in 1975. 10 October 1992.

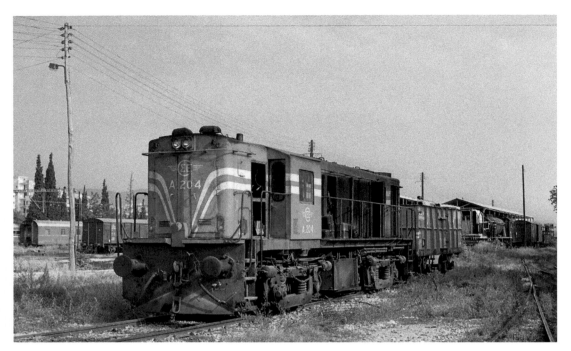

OSE Bo-Bo diesel-electric A.204 stands at Thessaloniki locomotive depot. Ten of these 1,050-hp locomotives, model DL532B, were built in 1962 by ALCo for the Hellenic State Railways. They were later rebuilt with low short hoods. 10 October 1992.

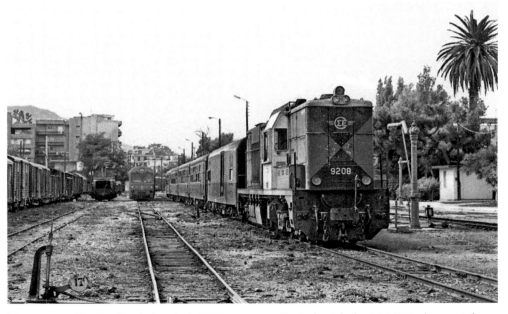

Metre gauge Co-Co diesel-electric A.9208 pauses at Corinth with the 06.10 Pirghos to Athens. Ten of these 1,600-hp locomotives were built by Alsthom in 1967 for the Hellenic State Railways. 6 October 1992.

Hungary

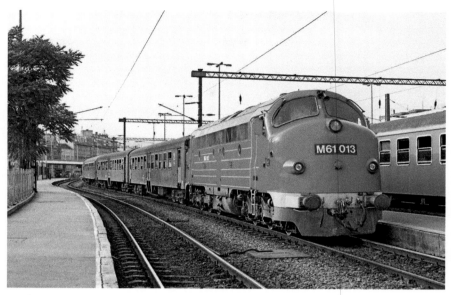

Magyar Államvasutak (MÁV) Co-Co diesel-electric M61 No. 013 waits for departure time at Budapest Déli with the 18.10 to Tapolca. This 1,950-hp locomotive was one of twenty built for MÁV by Nydqvist & Holm AB, under licence from General Motors, between 1963 and 1964. 5 June 1993.

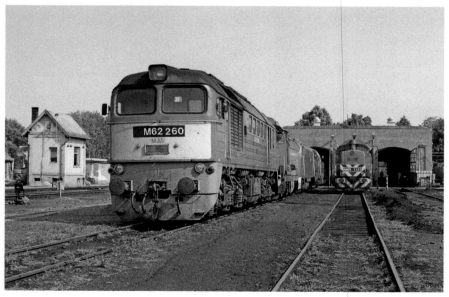

MÁV Co-Co diesel-electric M62 No. 260 stands at the front of a line of locomotives, including an M61, at Tapolca locomotive depot. Between 1965 and 1978, 294 Class M62 locomotives were built at Lugansk, Ukraine, for MÁV. B-B diesel-hydraulic shunter M43 No. 1125, built by FAUR, Romania, is on the right. 8 June 1993.

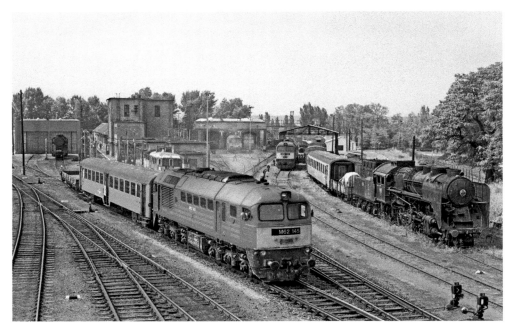

MÁV Co-Co diesel-electric M62 No. 145, built at the Voroshilovgrad locomotive factory, Lugansk, shunts at Celldömölk locomotive depot, Hungary. Other M62s are visible in the background, as well as an M41. The two steam locomotives are 424 Class 4-8-0s. 9 June 1993.

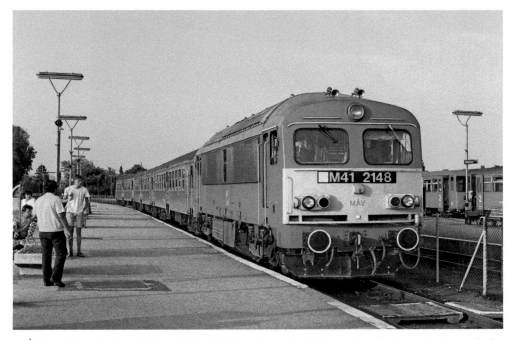

MÁV B-B diesel-hydraulic M41 No. 2148 is pictured at Balatonfüred, after arriving with the 17.47 from Székesfehérvár. Around 100 of these 1,800-hp locomotives were built for MÁV by Ganz-Mávag between 1972 and 1984. 8 June 1993.

India

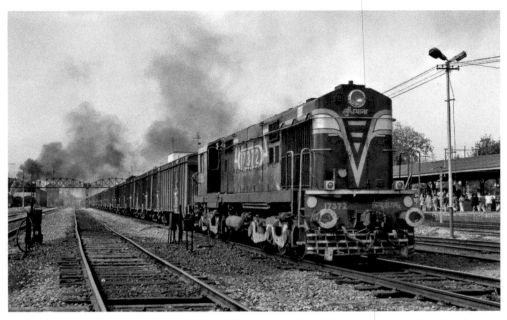

Indian Railways broad gauge Co-Co diesel-electric WDM2 No. 17372 waits with a freight train at Saharanpur station in northern India. The 2,600-hp WDM2 was developed in 1962 by ALCo, model DL560C, for the Indian Railways. More than 2,000 were built between 1962 and 1998 by ALCo and the Diesel Locomotive Works (DLW), Varanasi, India. 15 February 1994.

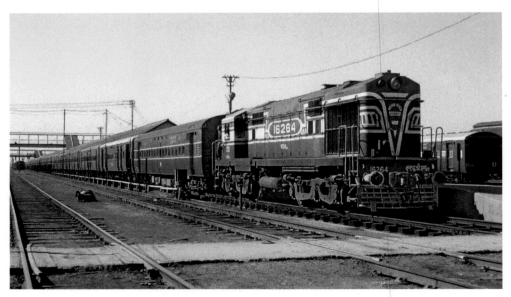

Indian Railways Co-Co diesel-electric WDM2 No. 16264, based at Andal diesel shed, waits for departure time with a passenger train at Gorakhpur. 15 February 1994.

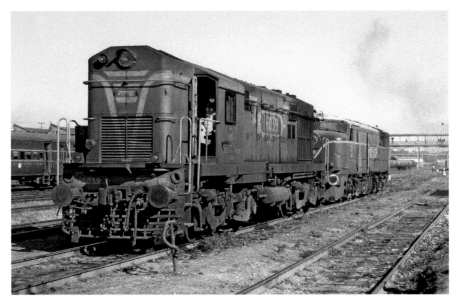

Co-Co diesel-electric WDM2 No. 16039 and WDM1 No. 17020 are pictured between duties at Gorakhpur. W stands for wide or broad gauge, D for diesel, and M for mixed traffic locomotive. The arrival of the Class WDM2 and later Class WDM4 saw the WDM1 locomotives relegated to secondary duties. 18 February 1994.

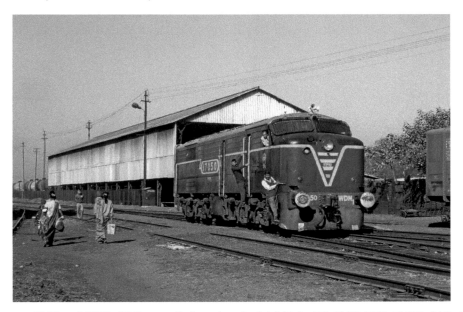

Between 1957 and 1959, ALCo supplied one hundred 1,950-hp DL500C (FPD-7) 'World Series' Co-Co diesel-electric locomotives to Indian Railways. Among the depots to receive allocations was Gorakhpur on the North Eastern Railway, in the Indian state of Uttar Pradesh. In 1994, WDM1 locomotives were still working around Gorakhpur and WDM1 No. 17050, allocated to Gonda diesel depot, is pictured shunting there. The ladies on the left appear to be attracting some attention from the crew of the locomotive! 18 February 1994.

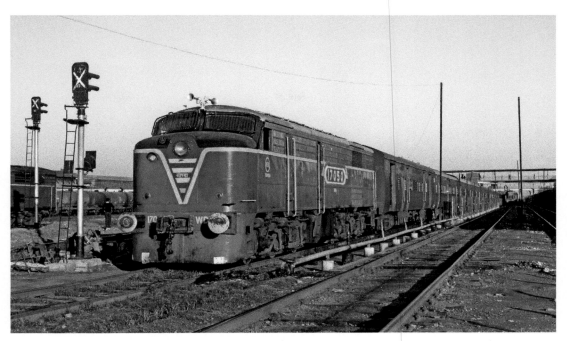

On a fine sunny day, WDM1 No. 17050 waits with a passenger train for departure time at Gorakhpur. 18 February 1994.

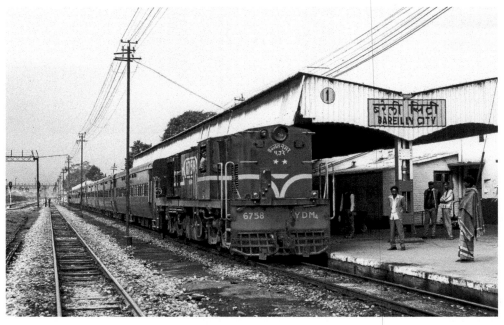

Metre gauge Co-Co diesel-electric YDM4 No. 6758 pauses with a passenger train at Bareilly City railway station. The first 1,350-hp YDM4 locomotives in India were imported from ALCo (model DL535) in 1961, but most were built by DLW, Varanasi, India. Around 800 locomotives of this type were constructed. 16 February 1994.

Ireland

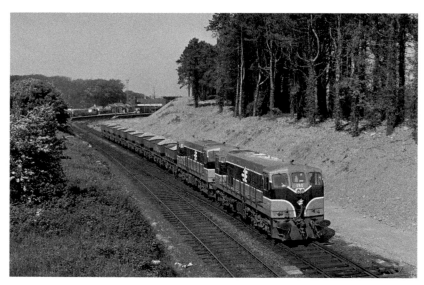

Irish Rail Class 181 Bo-Bo diesel-electrics Nos 190 and 183 pass Drogheda with a loaded ballast train from Dundalk. In 1966, twelve Class 181 locomotives, model JL18, were supplied to Córas Iompair Éireann (CIE) by General Motors. The locomotives were a development of the Class 141, fitted with a more powerful EMD 8-645E engine of 1,100 hp. 15 June 1996.

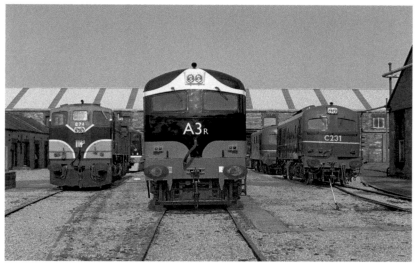

To celebrate the 150th anniversary of Inchicore Works, an open day was held in 1996. A variety of current and former motive power was on display. Here, GM Class 071 Co-Co diesel-electric No. 074 of 1977, Metropolitan Vickers Class 001 Co-Co diesel-electric A3r (previously No. 003) of 1955, and Metropolitan Vickers Class 201 Bo-Bo diesel-electric C231 of 1958 stand at the works. Bo-Bo diesel-electric B113, built at Inchicore Works in 1950 and fitted with a Sulzer engine, is behind. 15 June 1996.

Italy

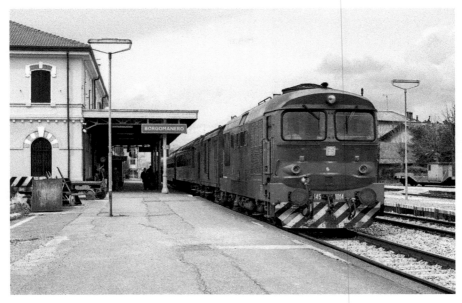

Ferrovie dello Stato (FS) Bo-Bo diesel-electric D.345 No. 1014 waits at Borgomanero with the 12.53 Domodossola to Novara. Between 1970 and 1979, 145 of these 1,350-hp locomotives were built for FS by Fiat at Breda and Officine Ferroviarie SpA (SOFER). 12 April 1998.

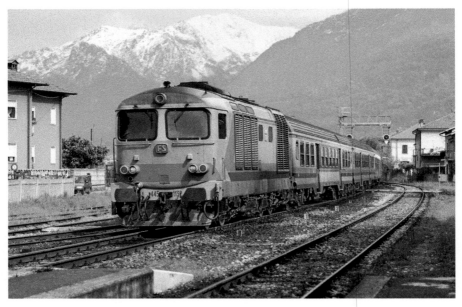

With a backdrop of the Alps, FS Bo-Bo diesel-electric D.445 No. 1132 arrives at Borgofranco d'Ivrea with the 08.40 Aosta to Torino. Between 1974 and 1988, 150 of these 2,000-hp locomotives were built by Fiat for FS. 18 April 1998.

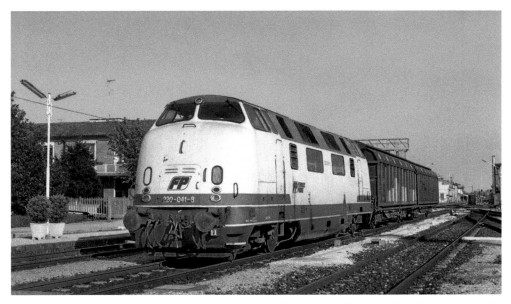

On the Ferrovie Padane (FP) from Ferrara to Codigoro, B-B diesel-hydraulic No. 220.041 stands at Ferrara station with a short freight to Codigoro. The locomotive is one of two V200.0 locomotives, later Class 220, that were sold by the Deutsche Bundesbahn to FP in 1984. Five V200 prototypes were built by Krauss-Maffei for DB in 1953 and 1954 followed by eighty-one production locomotives between 1956 and 1958, sixty-one by Krauss-Maffei and twenty by MaK. They were fitted with two V12 diesel engines producing a total of 2,170 hp. 14 April 1998.

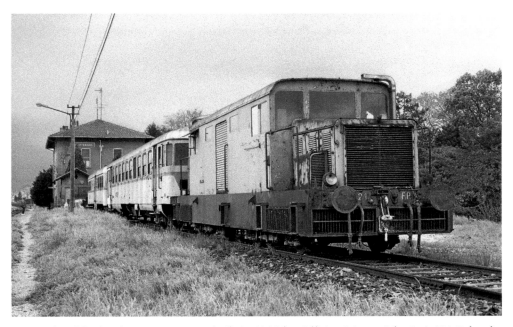

FP B-B diesel-hydraulic Ln No. 372.1, built in 1942 by Officine Meccaniche SpA (OM) for the war in Libya, stands at Quartesana station on the Ferrovie Padane. The locomotive never went to Libya and was sold by FS to the FP, where it remained in service until the 1990s. 15 April 1998.

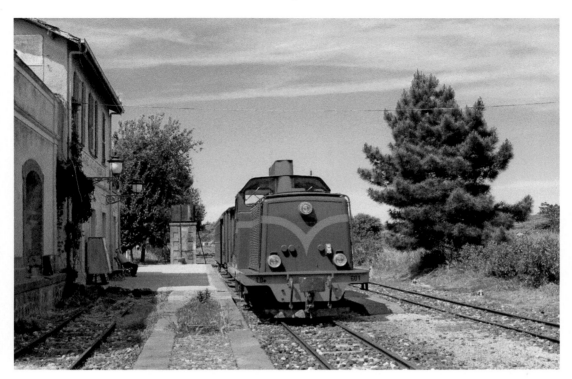

The Ferrovie della Sardegna is a 950-mm narrow gauge railway system on the Italian island of Sardinia. Most of the network is diesel operated using a mixture of diesel units and locomotive hauled trains. Here, Bo-Bo diesel-electric LDe No. 601 breaks its journey with a Railway Touring Company special train at Tresnuraghes. Introduced in 1958, the LDe class locomotives, built by Breda, were fitted with two 350-hp engines. 15 May 2006.

Indonesia

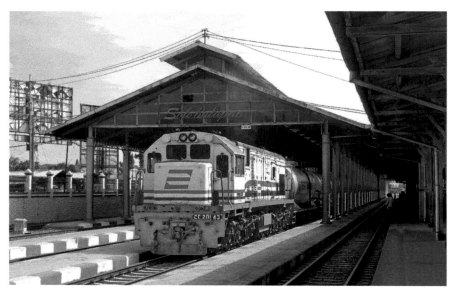

PT Kereta Api Indonesia (Persero) (KAI) is the Indonesian Railways Company. Here, KAI Co-Co diesel-electric CC201 No. 43 runs through Solo Balapan station, in the city of Surakarta, Central Java, with an eastbound tank train. Between 1976 and 1992, ninety-two of these 1,950-hp locomotives, model U18C, were built by General Electric Transportation, USA, for KAI. 24 July 2010.

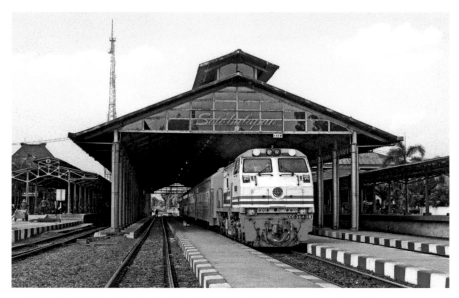

General Electric Co-Co diesel-electric CC204 No. 08 starts a westbound passenger train out of Solo Balapan station. Between 2006 and 2010, thirty of these 2,150-hp locomotives, model C20MP, were built by PT Industri Kereta Api (Persero), under licence from GE Transportation, for KAI. 24 July 2010.

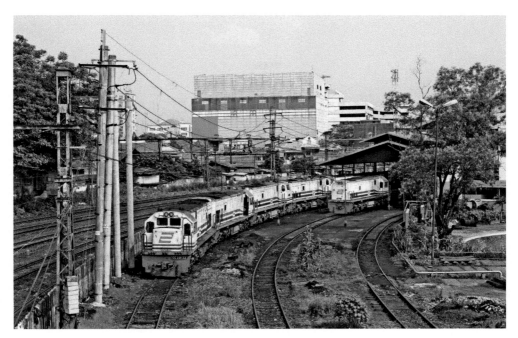

General Electric CC201 No. 22 stands at the front of a line of similar locomotives at Jakarta Jatinegara locomotive depot, Java. Another GE, CC201 No. 42, is on the right. The depot services Indonesian Railways diesel-electric locomotives. 9 August 2010.

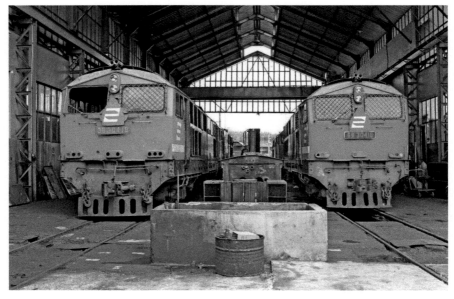

Jakarta Tanah Abang locomotive depot maintains Indonesian Railways diesel-hydraulic locomotives. Here, B-B diesel-hydraulics BB304 No. 19 and BB304 No. 18 are pictured inside the shed. Between 1976 and 1984, twenty-five of these 1,550-hp diesel-hydraulic locomotives, model M1500BB, were supplied to KAI by Krupp of Essen. They are similar to the 1501 Class locomotives in Thailand. 9 August 2010.

Luxembourg

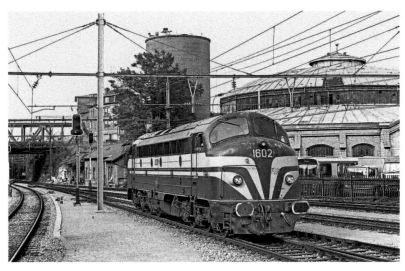

In 1955 Société Anglo-Franco-Belge of Belgium built four Co-Co diesel-electric locomotives for the Luxembourg Railways (Chemins de Fer Luxembourgeois or CFL), under a licence from General Motors EMD. Almost identical to the Belgian 202 class, these locomotives, designed for local passenger duties, were originally intended for Belgium. Here, CFL No. 1602 runs into Luxembourg station past one of the roundhouses at Luxembourg locomotive depot. The locomotive has since been preserved. 19 June 1992.

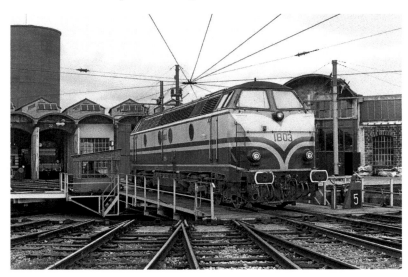

CFL Co-Co diesel-electric No. 1803 was a member of a class of twenty locomotives supplied to CFL in 1963. Fitted with GM 16-567C engines of 1,950 hp, they were built by La Brugeoise et Nivelles under a licence from Anglo-Franco-Belge to manufacture GM EMD locomotives for the European market. The class was a development of the CFL 1600 type and was similar to the SNCB Class 55. Here, No. 1803 is pictured on the turntable at Luxembourg locomotive depot. 19 June 1992.

Malaysia

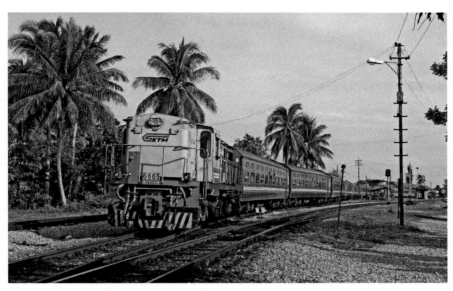

Keretapi Tanah Melayu Berhad (KTM) YDM4 No. 6665 shunts passenger stock at Tumpat, the terminus of the Jungle Line from Gemas. The 1,350-hp YDM4 Co-Co diesel-electric locomotives, ALCo model DL535A, were built between 1961 and 1990 for the Indian metre gauge railways by ALCo and DLW. In 2020, these locomotives were in use in the South East Asian countries of Cambodia, Myanmar and Vietnam. 23 January 2009.

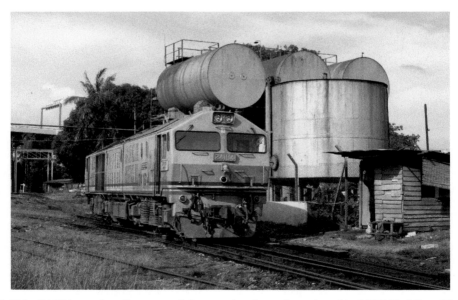

KTM No. 24104 stands at Butterworth locomotive depot. Introduced in 1987, Toshiba of Japan built twenty-six of these Co-Co diesel-electric locomotives for the Malaysian railways. They are fitted with Pielstick SP16 PA4V 200 VG engines of 2400 hp. 12 April 2009.

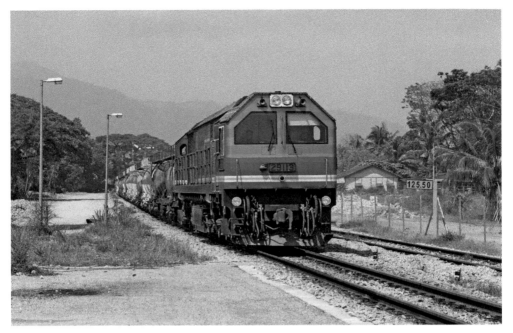

KTM No. 29113 heads a train of cement tanks from the YTL cement works at Padang Rengas south through Kuala Kangsar. From 2005, twenty of these Co-Co diesel-electric locomotives, model CKD8E fitted with 3,500-hp MAN 16RK215T engines, were built by Dalian, China, for KTM. 9 March 2010.

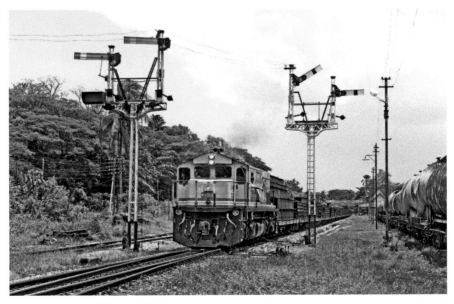

KTM Co-Co diesel-electric No. 25107 heads a steel train for the south, away from Bukit Mertajam. Seventeen of these Co-Co diesel-electric locomotives, classes 25/1 and 25/2, were built for KTM by General Motors, Canada, in 1990 (25/1) and 1998 (25/2). They are fitted with GM 8-645-E3C engines of 1,500 hp. 10 April 2009.

Myanmar

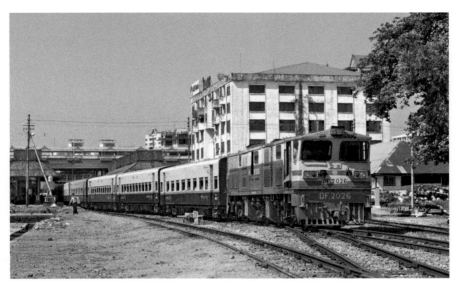

Myanmar Railways Bo-Bo-Bo diesel-electric DF.2026 heads the 11.00 to Shwenyaung out of Yangon station. The locomotive was built by Dalian, China, in 1993 and is fitted with a Caterpillar 3516DI-TA engine producing around 2,000 hp. 26 November 2018.

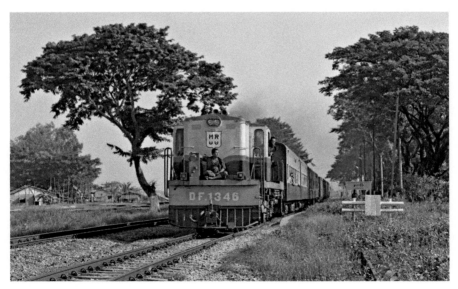

Myanmar Railways Co-Co diesel-electric DF.1346 heads a southbound mixed train from Mandalay through Ywathagyi. The locomotive is a refurbished ex-Indian Railways 1,350-hp YDM4 supplied through Rail India Technical and Economic Services Ltd (RITES). The work was carried out in India at the Golden Rock Railway Workshop in Ponmalai, Tiruchirappalli. The railwayman sitting on the front of the locomotive appears to be enjoying the ride, despite the relatively high speed of the train. 24 November 2018.

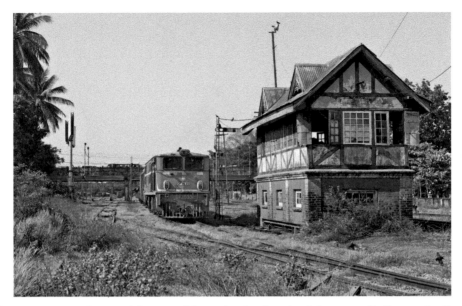

After arriving at Bago with a southbound mixed train, Myanmar Railways Bo-Bo-Bo diesel-electric DF.1635 shunts freight wagons into Bago yard past the mechanical signal box at the south end of the station. This 1,600-hp locomotive was built by Alsthom in the 1970s. Some locomotives of this class have been fitted with replacement engines from Jinan Diesel Engine Co. Ltd, China. 6 March 2019.

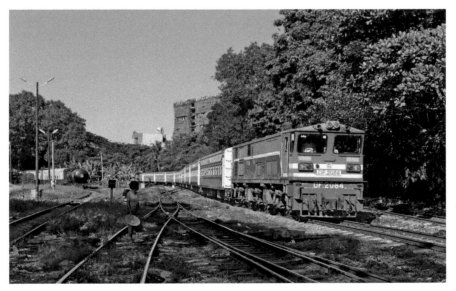

Myanmar Railways diesel-electric DF.2084 heads the 15.00 to Yangon past the carriage sheds as it departs from Mandalay. Because of Myanmar's tight curves and steep gradients this modern 2,000-hp Dalian locomotive, type CKD7B, runs on three two-axle bogies instead of the more usual two three-axle arrangement, so the wheel arrangement is Bo-Bo-Bo or tri-Bo. Locomotives of this class are now being assembled in Myanmar, in co-operation with CRRC Dalian, at a recently completed locomotive factory in Naypyitaw. 1 December 2018.

The Netherlands

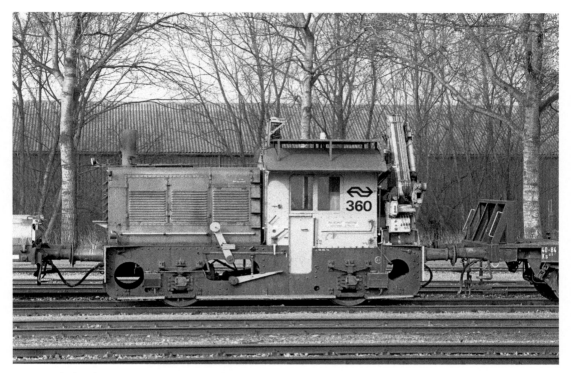

Nederlandse Spoorwegen (NS) Class 200 0-4-0 diesel-electric No. 360, fitted with a Hiab telescopic crane, is pictured at Geldermalsen. Between 1934 and 1951, 169 of these shunting locomotives were built by Werkspoor, of which fifteen were rebuilt with a retractable crane. 7 April 1996.

Norway

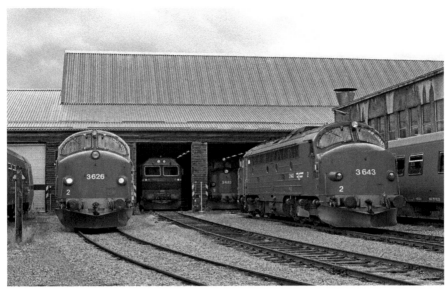

Norges Statsbaner (NSB) diesel-electric locomotives Co-Co Di3a No. 626, Co-Co Di4 No. 654, Co-Co Di3a No. 633 and A1A-A1A Di3b No. 643 stand at Marienborg locomotive depot, near Trondheim. 12 August 1992.

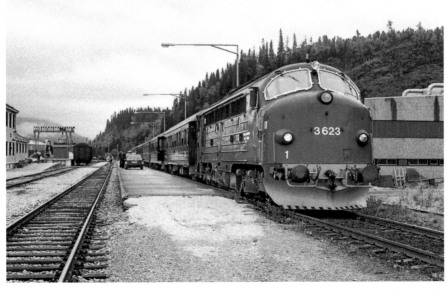

NSB NOHAB GM Co-Co diesel-electric Di3a No. 623 pauses at Trofors with the 08.30 Trondheim to Bodø. Between 1954 and 1969, thirty-five Class Di3 locomotives, fitted with EMD 16-567 engines of 1,775 hp, were supplied to NSB by Nydqvist & Holm AB, under licence from General Motors. 10 August 1992.

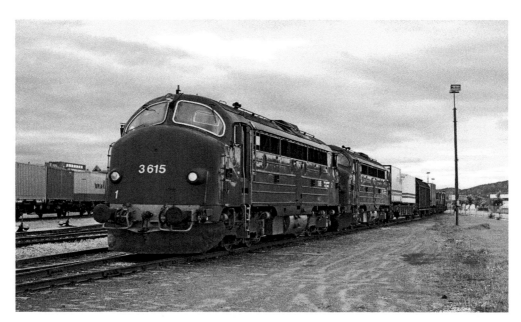

NSB NOHAB GM diesel-electrics Di3a No. 615 and Di3a No. 604 wait in the yard at Bodø with a mixed freight to Trondheim. Between 1989 and 1993, the No. 1 end cabs of many of these locomotives were upgraded, with the modifications including stronger windscreens, as can be seen on Di3a No. 615. The No. 2 end of Di3a No. 604, behind, is facing the camera and the old windscreen with a protective metal grille is visible. 10 August 1992.

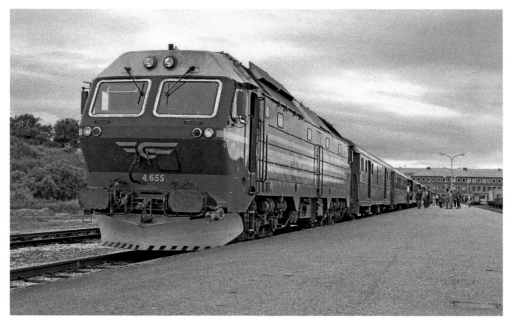

NSB Co-Co diesel-electric Di4 No. 655 waits for departure time at Bodø with the 20.35 to Trondheim, including sleeping coaches. In 1981, five of these 3,290-hp Class Di4 diesel-electric locomotives were built for NSB by Henschel, Germany, for use on the Nordland line. 10 August 1992.

Pakistan

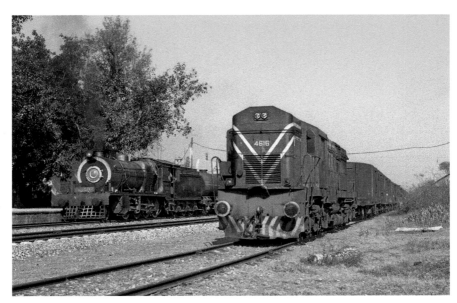

Pakistan Railways (PR) ALU24 Class Co-Co diesel-electric No. 4616, one of a class of twenty 2,400-hp ALCo DL560 export locomotives introduced in 1967, stands at Khairabad Kund station. HGS Class 2-8-0 steam locomotive No. 2303 is alongside. 31 December 1997.

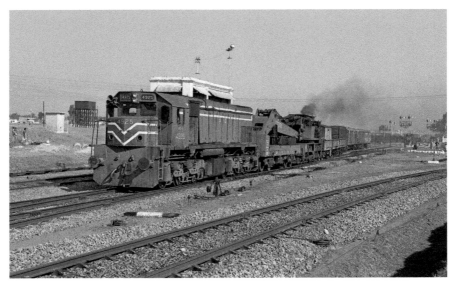

Pakistan Railways 1,500-hp GMCU15 Class Co-Co diesel-electric No. 4925, General Motors type GL-22-CU introduced in 1979, heads a westbound breakdown train, including a steam crane, away from Attock City Junction railway station. The crane, based at Rawalpindi, was one of a batch of four 65-ton breakdown cranes produced by Cowans Sheldon for Pakistan and is No. 395, built in 1966. 31 December 1998.

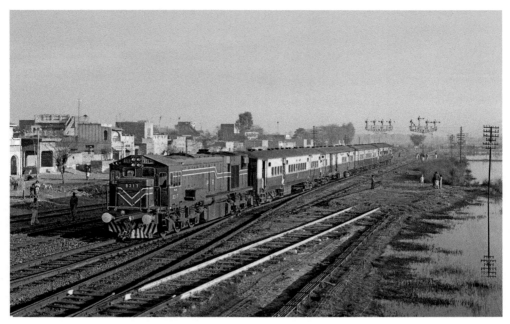

Pakistan Railways PHA20 Class Co-Co diesel-electric No. 8317, Hitachi model DE2200, built at the Pakistan Locomotive Factory, Risalpur, in 1990, heads train 33 from Lahore to Faisalabad into Chak Jhumra station, near Faisalabad. The locomotive is one of twenty-three of this type and is fitted with an ALCo 12-251C4 engine of 2,200 hp. 3 January 1998.

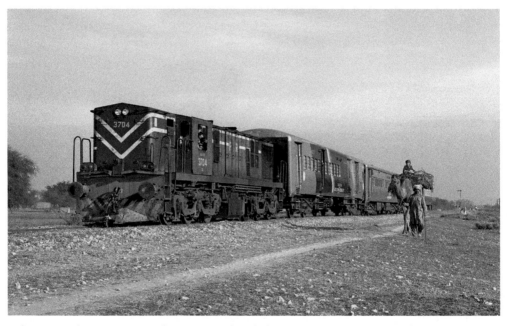

Pakistan Railways ALU12 Class Co-Co diesel-electric No. 3704, a 1,350-hp ALCo DL535 export locomotive, heads a special train, organised by Steam & Safaris, between Malakwal and Khewra. Note the camel on the right. 4 January 1998.

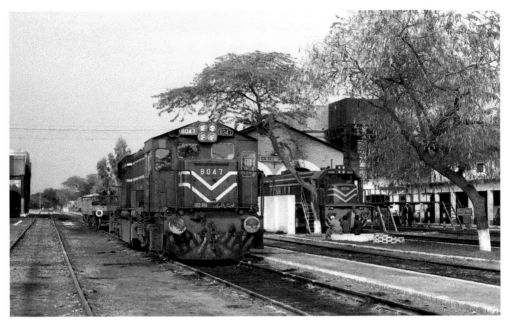

Pakistan Railways Hitachi HBU20 2,000-hp Co-Co diesel-electric No. 8047 and GRU20 2,000-hp Co-Co diesel-electric No. 5006, type C20-7i built at the Pakistan Locomotive Factory, Mogulpura, are pictured at Sibi Junction locomotive depot. 7 January 1998.

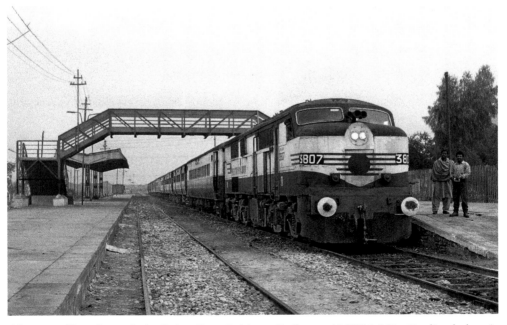

After travelling through the Bolān Pass, Pakistan Railways ALPW 16 Co-Co diesel-electric No. 3807 pauses at Sehwan Sharif station with a southbound express from Quetta. This is a 1,600-hp DL500C export locomotive built by ALCo Products Inc, USA. The class entered service in Pakistan in 1956. 9 January 1998.

Peru

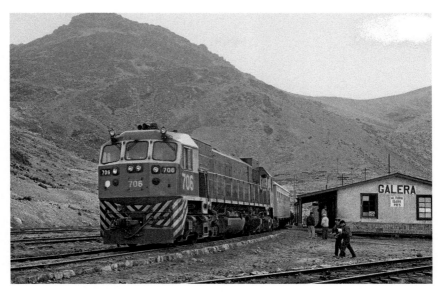

Ferrocarril Central Andino Co-Co diesel-electric No. 706 stands at Galera station after arriving with a special train from Lima, organised by Along Different Lines (ADL). As can be seen on the station sign, Galera is 15,681 feet above sea level. The locomotive, a General Motors model JT26CW-2B, is based on the EMD SD40-2 and was built in 1988 by Villares in Brazil for Enafer SA. 18 November 1999.

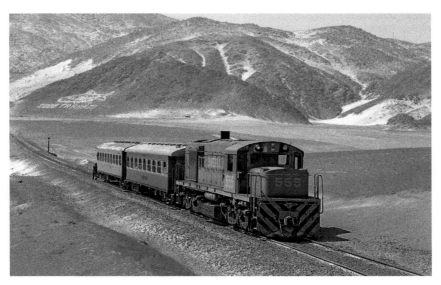

Enafer SA ALCo DL543 Co-Co diesel-electric No. 555, built in 1961, heads a charter train, organised by ADL, from Arequipa to Mollendo and Matarani, Peru. It is pictured here in the desert between Arequipa and Mollendo. The ALCo DL543 export locomotives were fitted with 12-251C engines of around 2,000 hp. 27 November 1999.

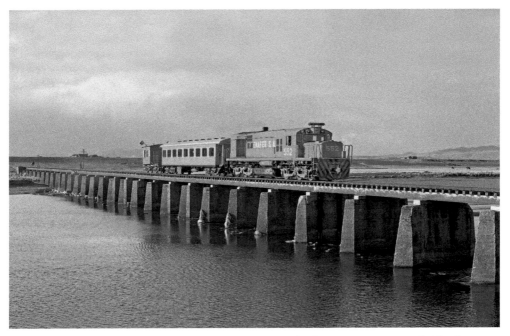

Enafer SA Alco DL543 Co-Co diesel-electric No. 552, built in 1961, crosses a bridge between La Raya and Juliaca, with an ADL charter train from Cusco to Puno. Note the lights on the cab roof of the locomotive that look as if they have come from a police car. 25 November 1999.

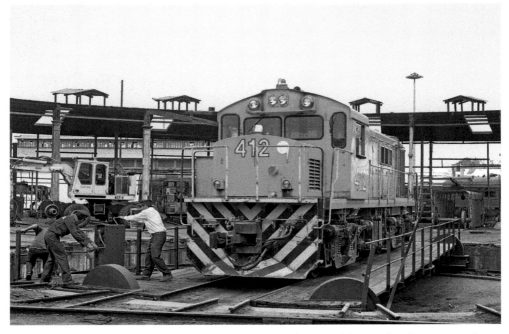

Enafer SA Bo-Bo diesel-electric No. 412 is pictured on the turntable at Callao locomotive depot, Lima, Peru. The locomotive is a 1,200-hp DL532B, built by MLW. 29 November 1999.

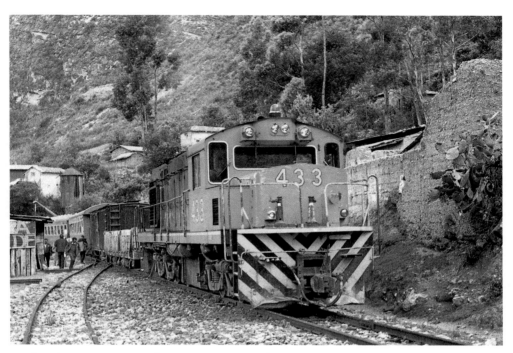

On the 3 feet gauge Ferrocarril Huancayo-Huancavelica (FHH), ALCo DL515B Co-Co diesel-electric No. 433, built in 1963, waits at a passing loop with the 06.30 Huancayo to Huancavelica. The line was converted to standard gauge between 2006 and 2010. 20 November 1999.

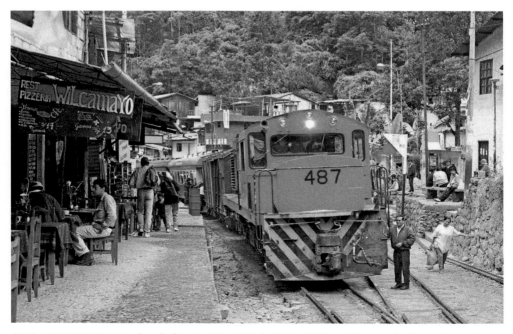

ALCo DL535B Co-Co diesel-electric No. 487, built in 1963 and later rebuilt, waits at Aguas Calientes, the station for Machu Picchu, with the 17.30 to Cusco. 24 November 1999.

Poland

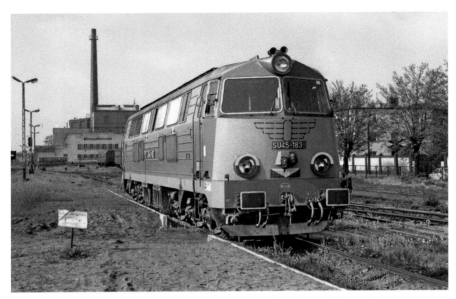

Polskie Koleje Państwowe (PKP) 1,750-hp Co-Co diesel-electric SU45.183 is pictured stabled at Leszno. The 191 Class SU45 locomotives, fitted with electric train heating, were rebuilt from Class SP45 locomotives between 1987 and 1998. The Class SP45 was built by Cegielski at Poznań, Poland, between 1970 and 1976. 11 May 1995.

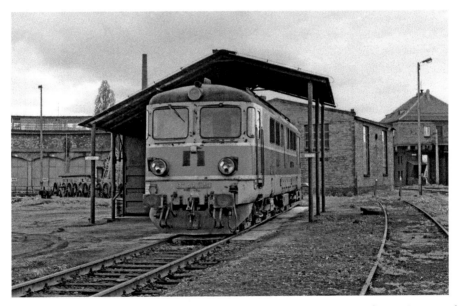

PKP Co-Co diesel-electric ST43.229, fitted with a Sulzer 12LDA28 2,100-hp engine, stands at Gniezno locomotive depot. Between 1965 and 1978, 422 of these locomotives were built by Electroputere, Craiova, Romania, for freight duties. 10 May 1995.

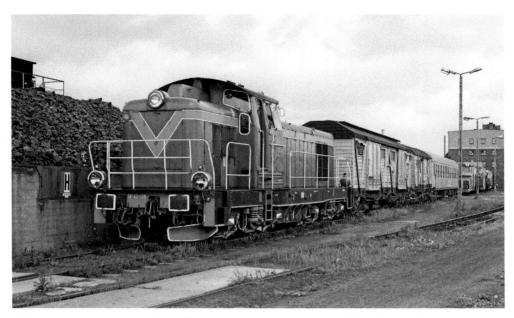

PKP Bo-Bo diesel-electric SP42.108 is pictured at Leszno depot. The 800-hp SP42 was built by Fablok at Chrzanów, Poland, model Ls800, between 1967 and 1972. It was a passenger version of the SM42 Class equipped with steam heating. 11 May 1995.

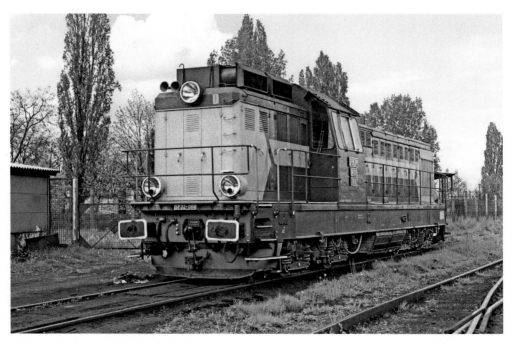

PKP Bo-Bo diesel-electric SP32.088 at Zbąszynek locomotive depot. Between 1985 and 1991, 150 of these 957-hp passenger locomotives, fitted with electric train heating, were built by FAUR, Bucharest, Romania. Reliability problems resulted in various modifications being made to the class. FAUR was previously the 23 August locomotive works. 11 May 1995.

Portugal

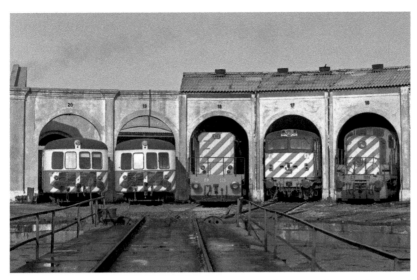

Barreiro locomotive depot, situated across the Tagus from Lisboa, was the main locomotive depot for southern Portugal. Here, an assortment of motive power stands in the semi-roundhouse at Barreiro. Two NOHAB railcars are on the left, and the diesel-electric locomotives are Montreal Locomotive Works (MLW) Co-Co No. 1568, English Electric Co-Co No. 1806, and ALCo A1A-A1A No. 1524. 16 March 1992.

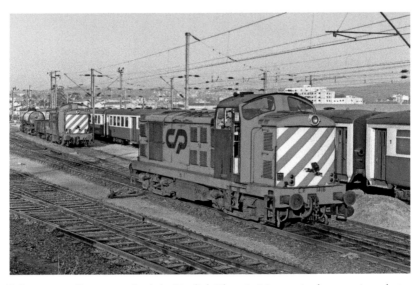

Contumil depot, near Porto, serviced the English Electric 14xx series locomotives that were used on trains on the Northern and Douro Valley lines. Here, English Electric Bo-Bo diesel-electrics Nos 1416 and 1457 stand at Contumil. Between 1967 and 1969, sixty-seven of these locomotives, fitted with 1,330-hp 8CSVT engines, were built by English Electric at the Vulcan Foundry and by Sociedades Reunidas de Fabricações Metálicas (SOREFAME), Portugal. 19 March 1992.

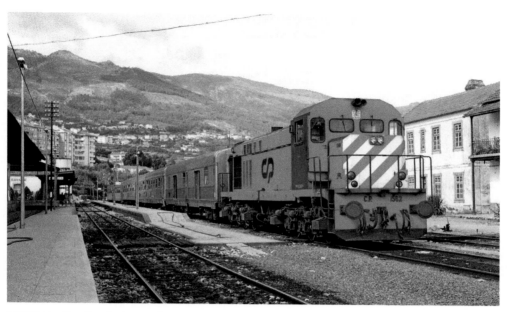

MLW Co-Co diesel-electric locomotive No. 1562 stands at Covilhã with the 15.55 train to Lisboa Santa Apolónia. Introduced in 1973, twenty of these 2,000-hp MX-620 locomotives, fitted with ALCo 251-C3 engines, were supplied to Caminhos de Ferro Portugueses (CP) by the Montreal Locomotive Works. 17 September 1996.

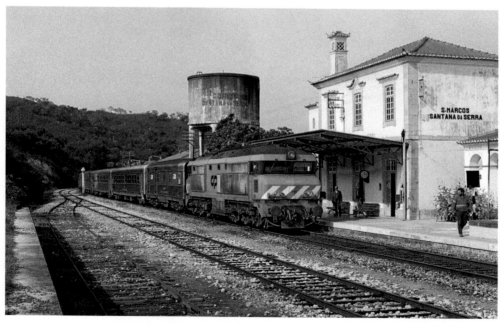

Co-Co diesel-electric No. 1935 arrives at São Marcos da Serra with IR871, the 08.35 Barreiro to Vila Real de Santo António, on the border with Spain. Introduced in 1981, seventeen of these mixed traffic locomotives were built for CP by SOREFAME, under licence from Alsthom. 2 November 1999.

Russia

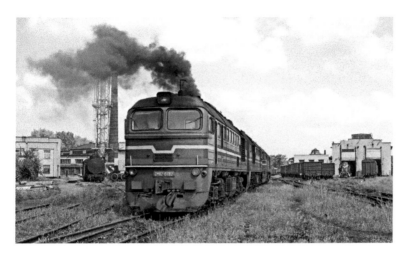

The first locomotive of Co-Co diesel-electric double locomotive 2M62 No. 0482, built at Lugansk, is started at Chernyakhovsk depot, Russia. As is the case with all the standard locomotive types, the M62, in its various forms, was used in very large numbers throughout the Soviet Union and, after its dissolution, throughout its former constituent countries. 6 June 1999.

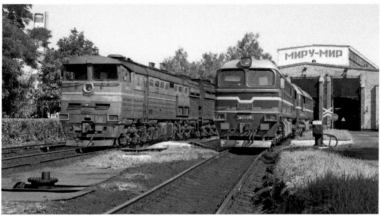

Co-Co diesel-electric double locomotives 2TE10M No. 0343 and 2M62U No. 0245 stand at Bryansk depot No. 2, Russia. The M62U is a version of the M62 with increased fuel capacity. 7 August 2000.

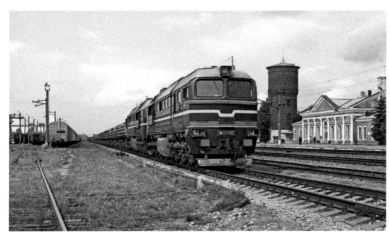

In maroon livery, Co-Co diesel-electric double locomotive 2M62U No. 0245 leads a freight train through Zhakovka, Russia. 8 August 2000.

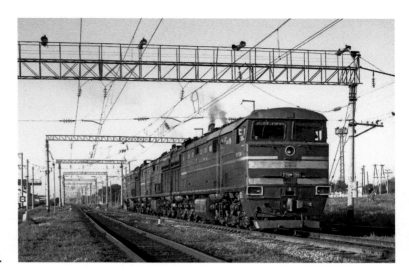

Co-Co diesel-electric triple locomotive 3TE10M No. 1268 is pictured at Kastornaya, Russia. 10 August 2000.

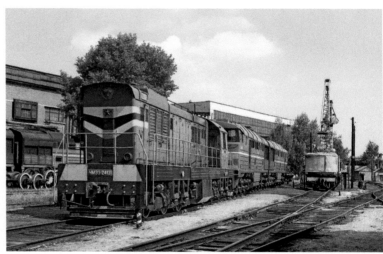

Co-Co diesel-electric CHME3 No. 2413, built by ČKD, stands at Beolograd locomotive depot, Russia. 12 August 2000.

Station pilot Co-Co diesel-electric TEM2 No. 1135 shunts empty stock at Kaliningrad station. Until 1946, Kaliningrad was named Königsberg, a large city located in eastern Germany. It is an exclave of the Russian Federation, detached from the rest of the country. 7 June 1999.

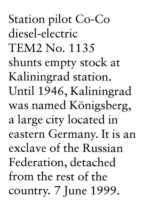

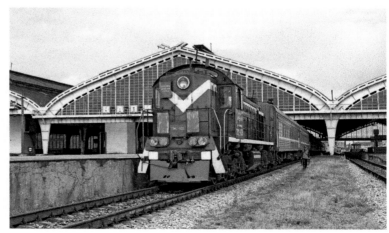

Serbia

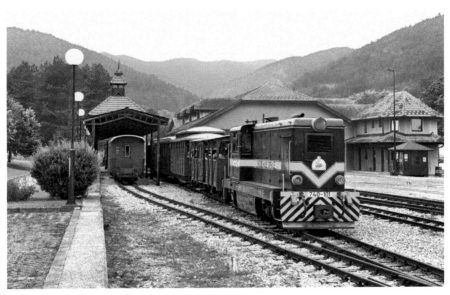

After travelling over the Šargan Eight, narrow gauge B-B diesel-hydraulic No. 740.101 arrives at Šargan Vitasi with a tourist train from Mokra Gora. The 760-mm gauge locomotive was built in 1970 by Đuro Đaković at Slavonski Brod. 17 June 2019.

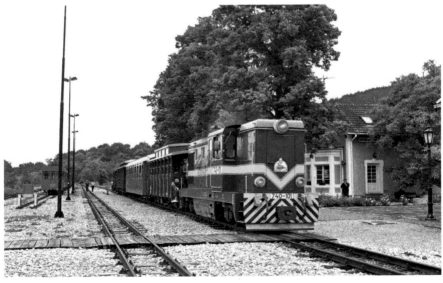

B-B diesel-hydraulic No. 740.101 departs from Šargan Vitasi with a train to Mokra Gora. The 760-mm gauge railway climbs from Mokra Gora (660 metres above sea level) to Šargan Vitasi (810 metres above sea level) by means of a series of curves in the shape of an 8, hence the name Šargan Eight. This spectacular section of railway was part of the former narrow gauge main line from Sarajevo to Belgrade. It is now operated for tourists. 17 June 2019.

Slovenia

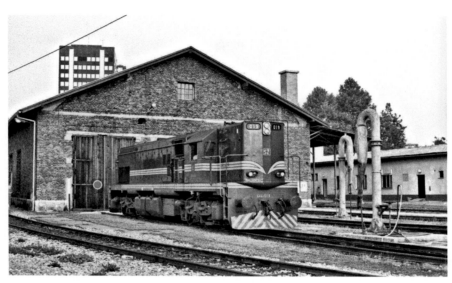

In 1973 and 1974, twenty-five 1,600-hp locomotives Nos 644.001 to 644.025, EMD model G22U, were supplied to Jugoslovenske Željeznice (JŽ) by Material y Construcciones SA (MACOSA), Spain. Here, after the breakup of Yugoslavia, Slovenske Železnice (SŽ) A1A-A1A diesel-electric No. 644.019 is pictured between duties at Ljubljana. 28 August 1999.

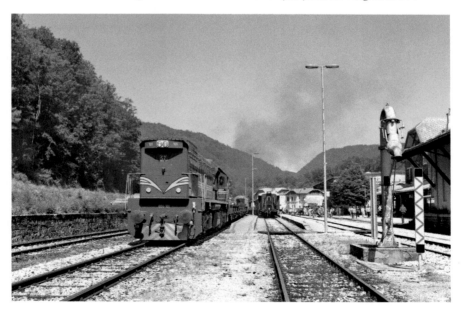

SŽ Co-Co diesel-electric No. 664.101 pauses at Most Na Soči with a northbound Trans Europ Motorail. Twenty of these 2,168-hp locomotives, EMD export model G26, were built by Đuro Đaković for JŽ as Class 664.1 and were transferred to SŽ after the breakup of Yugoslavia. 8 June 2019.

South Africa

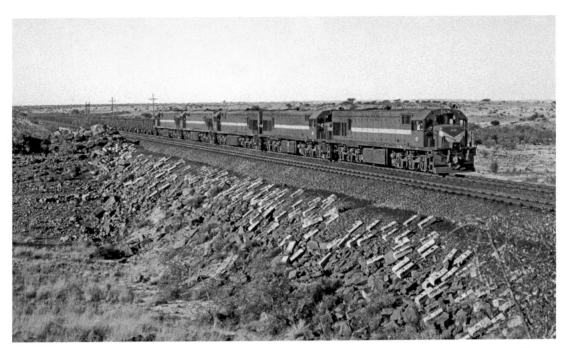

Five South African Railways Class 34.000 GE U26C Co-Co diesel-electric locomotives, in gulf red and whiskers livery and with No. 34.021 leading, head a heavy freight train near Witput, Republic of South Africa. Between 1971 and 1973, 125 of these 2,750-hp locomotives were built by GE and the South African General Electric-Dorman Long Locomotive Group for South African Railways. 5 October 1975.

Spain

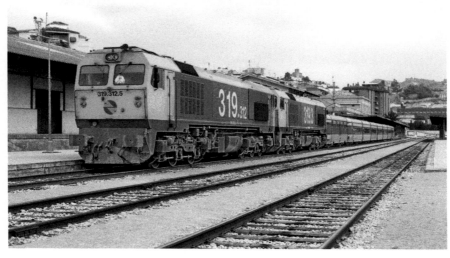

Red Nacional de los Ferrocarriles Españoles (RENFE) Co-Co diesel-electrics Nos 319.312 and 319.308 stand at Granada with the 15.40 Talgo to Madrid. In 1991 and 1992, forty 2,000-hp 319.3 locomotives were built for RENFE by Meinfesa, previously MACOSA, with components from GM. 3 September 1998.

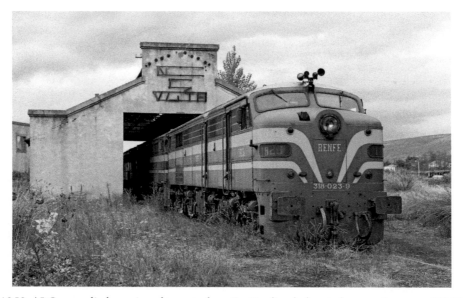

In 1958, ALCo supplied a series of twenty-four Co-Co diesel-electric locomotives, type DL500C (FPD-7), to RENFE. They were fitted with ALCo V12 251B engines of 1,980 hp. Here, RENFE ALCo DL500C No. 318.023, previously No. 1823, is pictured stored at Monforte de Lemos locomotive depot after withdrawal from service. 21 September 1993.

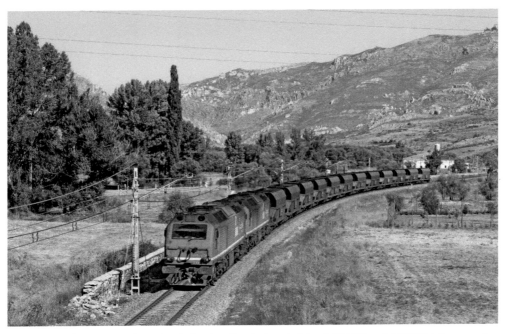

Acciona Rail Services Class 333.3 Co-Co diesel-electric No. 333.383, a MACOSA locomotive rebuilt with input from Alsthom, leads a second member of the class on a southbound coal train near Villamanin, Spain. Between 2000 and 2005, ninety-two of these locomotives were built for freight duties, using components from 2,500-hp Class 333 locomotives. Only the engines and generators were reused. 15 September 2007.

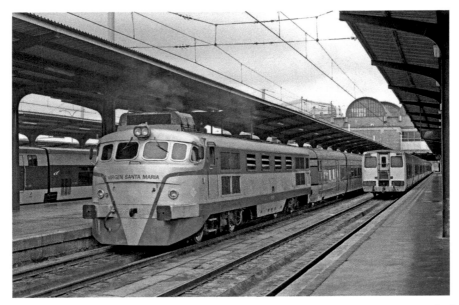

Talgo B-B 2,400-hp twin-engined diesel-hydraulic No. 352.006 *Virgen Santa Maria*, built by Babcock & Wilcox in 1965, waits for departure time at Madrid Chamartín station with the 15.45 Talgo service to Bilbao. 29 September 1998.

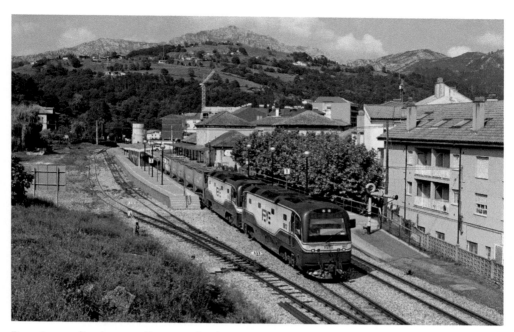

Running on diesel power, Ferrocarriles de Vía Estrecha (FEVE) metre gauge Bo-Bo electro-diesel locomotives Nos 1912 and 1908 head a westbound freight through Arriondas, Spain. Introduced in 2002, seventeen of these 1,500 V electric/diesel locomotives were built for FEVE, converted from Alsthom Class 1000 locomotives. 10 September 2007.

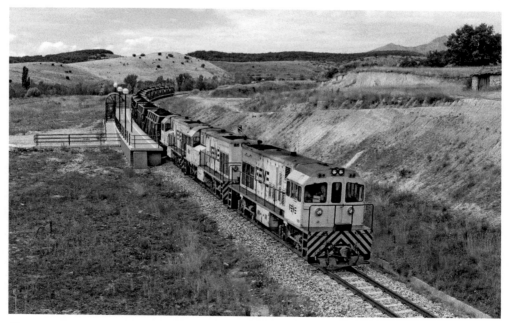

FEVE metre gauge Bo-Bo diesel-electric No. 1509 leads two other Class 1500 diesels on a loaded coal train through Prado de la Guzpeña station. The locomotives are GE model U10B and are fitted with Caterpillar 1,300-hp engines. 18 September 2007.

Thailand

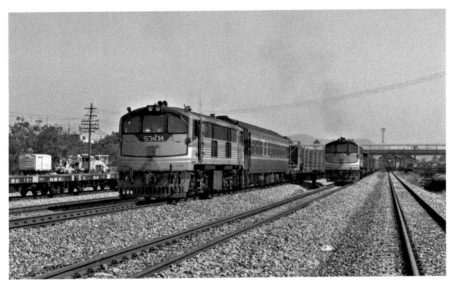

State Railway of Thailand (SRT) General Electric No. 4030 stands at the head of a westbound permanent way train at Kaeng Khoi Junction. A second GE, No. 4016, shunts a freight train alongside. GE built fifty of these Co-Co diesel-electric locomotives, model UM12C Shovel Nose, for SRT between 1963 and 1965. Fitted with two unsilenced Cummins engines developing a total of 1,320-hp, they are a favourite of many enthusiasts. 19 December 2018.

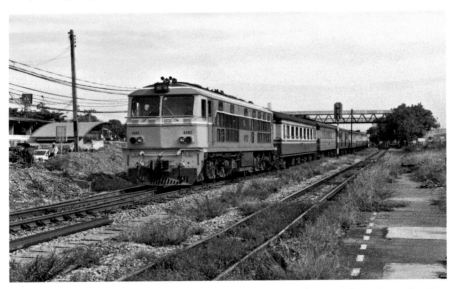

Alsthom No. 4102 heads train 170, the 12.35 Yala to Bangkok, away from Bang Sue Junction station, Bangkok. A total of 113 of these Co-Co diesel-electric locomotives, model AD24C, were built in four batches between 1974 and 1985 by Alsthom, Henschel and Krupp. The blue stripe carried by the locomotive indicates that it has been rebuilt with an MTU engine. 31 October 2019.

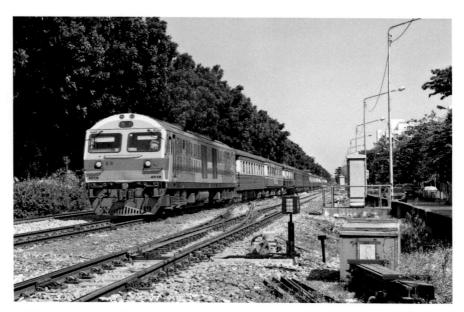

Hitachi No. 4519 nears the end of its journey as it passes Ramathipodi with train 172, the 11.30 Su-ngai Kolok to Bangkok. The locomotive is painted in a livery that matches the new Chinese sleepers that the class usually hauls. Twenty-two of these Co-Co diesel-electric locomotives, model 8FA-36C, were built by Hitachi in 1993. They are fitted with twin Cummins engines producing a total of 2,860 hp. 18 December 2019.

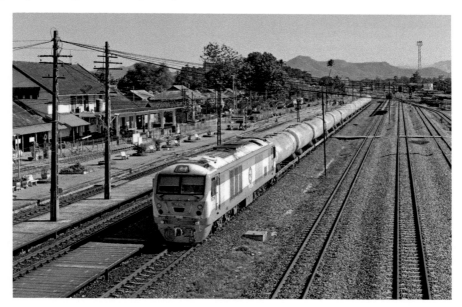

Co-Co diesel-electric No. 70102 runs through Kaeng Khoi Junction station with cement tanks from Hin Lap works to the cement terminal at Preng. The locomotive is one of twelve owned by TPI Polene PLC for hauling their trains from Hin Lap to cement terminals throughout Thailand. Built by CSR Zhiyang, China, these locomotives are fitted with Caterpillar 3516B HD engines producing 2,760 hp. 17 December 2018.

Turkey

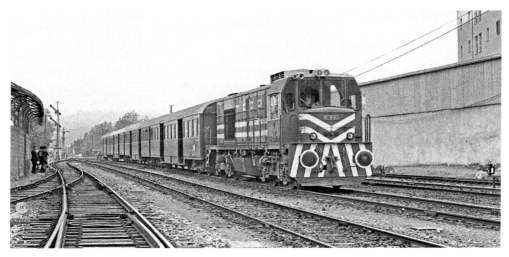

Turkish State Railways (Türkiye Cumhuriyeti Devlet Demiryollari or TCDD) Bo-Bo diesel-electric DE18.002, one of a class of five locomotives built in 1970 by Matériel de Traction Electrique, a joint venture between Jeumont-Schneider and Creusot-Loire, arrives at Izmir with a local train. These locomotives were fitted with Pielstick 12PA4 V185 VG engines producing 1,770 hp. 29 September 1977.

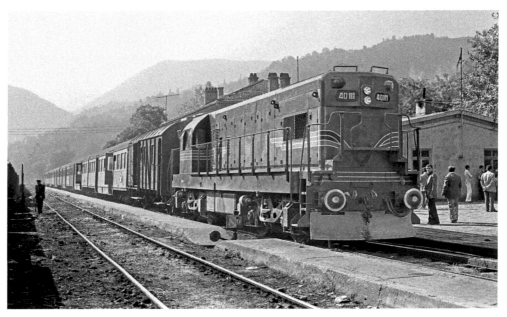

Iranian GM G12W Bo-Bo diesel-electric No. 40.111 stands at Zonguldak, Turkey, with a passenger train. This locomotive is one of 137 supplied to the Islamic Republic of Iran Railways and was on hire to TCDD at the time. The G12 locomotives were fitted with EMD 12-567C engines rated at 1,250 hp. 20 September 1977.

Ukraine

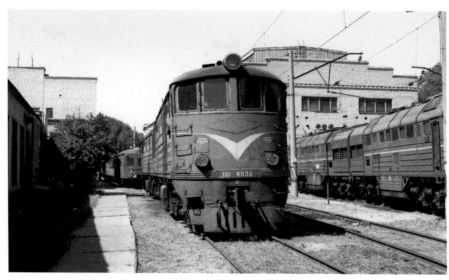

Co-Co diesel-electric double locomotive TE3 No. 4036 stands at Dnepropetrovsk Freight Depot, Ukraine. The TE3 was the first major diesel freight locomotive to work on the railways of the USSR. Prototypes were built from 1953 and full-scale production began in 1956, ending in 1973. Over 6,000 2 x 2000 hp units were built at Kharkov, Lugansk (Voroshilovgrad), Kolomna and Electrotyazhmash. The TE3 was the locomotive on which the Chinese DF was based. 14 June 1998.

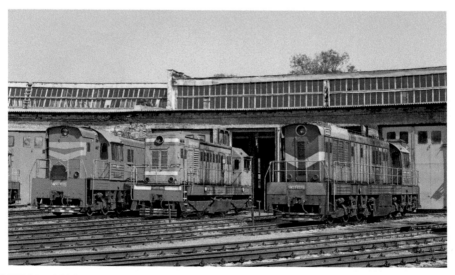

CHME3 No. 3020, CHME2 No. 196 and CHME3 No. 6370 stand outside the semi-roundhouse at Darnitsa depot, Ukraine. Over 500 CHME2 Bo-Bo diesel-electric shunting locomotives were built by ČKD in Czechoslovakia between 1957 and 1965. They were fitted with 6S310DR engines producing 750 hp. The CHME3 locomotives were also built by ČKD. 13 August 2000.

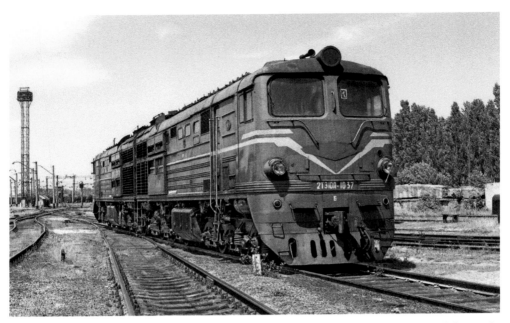

Co-Co diesel-electric double locomotive 2TE10L No. 1037, built at Lugansk (Voroshilovgrad), is pictured at Kharkov (Osnova) diesel depot, Ukraine. Between 1957 and 1961, a new, more powerful version of the TE3, the TEP 10, was developed for passenger duties. After 1961, work on the freight version of the new locomotive, the 2TE10L, was carried out at Lugansk. Note the rounded appearance of the front of the locomotive. Later versions of the TE10 were more angular. 11 June 1998.

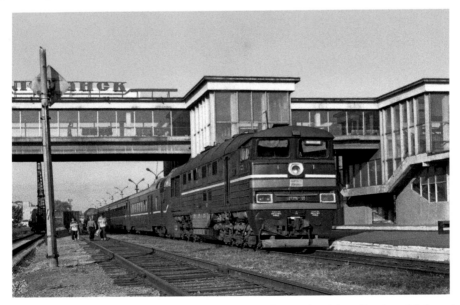

Half of 2TE116 No. 735 double locomotive waits at Lugansk with a diesel multiple unit on a local passenger service. The diesel unit was being used as coaching stock. A second half of a 2TE116 is on the rear of the train. 12 June 1998.

United Kingdom

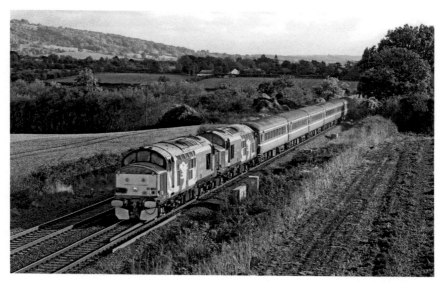

Rail Operations Group English Electric Co-Co diesel-electrics Nos 37800 and 37884 pass Defford, heading for Worcester, with 'The Class 37/8 Thrash Bash' rail tour from Derby to Worcester Shrub Hill. Between 1960 and 1965, 309 of these 1,750-hp locomotives were built for British Railways and were the railway's standard Type 3 locomotives. 23 October 2016.

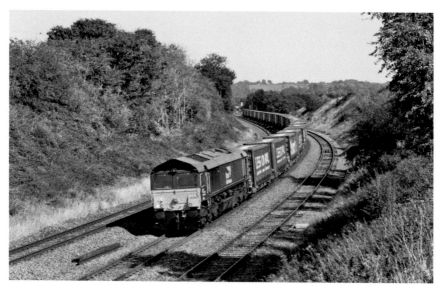

Direct Rail Services EMD Co-Co diesel-electric No. 66303 approaches Stoke Works Junction with a container train from Daventry to Wentloog. Between 1998 and 2015, 480 of these locomotives, EMD model JT42CWR fitted with 3,300-hp EMD 12N-710G3B-EC two-stroke diesel engines, were supplied to various operators in the UK. They are also used in various countries in Continental Europe. 14 September 2020.

United States of America

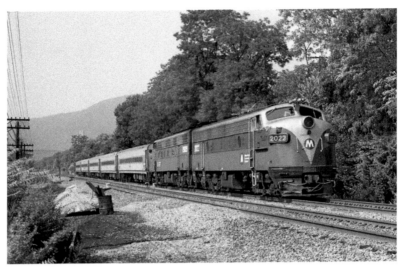

Metro-North Commuter Railroad FL9 Bo-A1A electro-diesel locomotives Nos 2022 and 2029 propel a commuter train, from Poughkeepsie to New York's Grand Central Terminal station, near Manitou. Sixty of these locomotives were built between 1956 and 1960 by General Motors Electro-Motive Division for the New York, New Haven and Hartford Railroad. They were fitted with EMD 567 engines and contact shoes to pick up power from the electrified third rail around Grand Central Terminal. 2 August 1993.

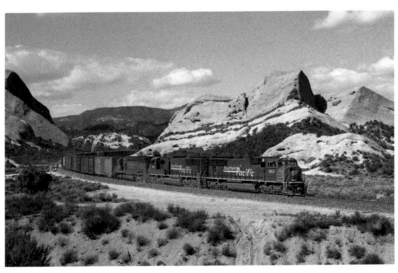

Southern Pacific EMD SD70M Co-Co diesel-electrics Nos 9802 and 9801 and an unidentified EMD SD40-2 head a westbound freight at Cajon Junction, California, USA. Introduced in 1992, large numbers of various versions of the SD70 have been built, including 1,609 SD70Ms between 1992-2004. They are fitted with EMD 16-710-G3 two-stroke engines producing 4,000 hp. 1 April 1995.

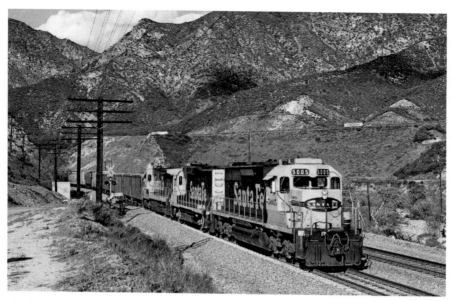

Santa Fe EMD SD40u Co-Co diesel-electric No. 5005 and two other SD40s head a westbound mixed freight at Blue Cut, Cajon Pass, California, USA. SD40u No. 5005 is a 3,000-hp SD40, built in 1966 and rebuilt in 1981. 2 April 1995.

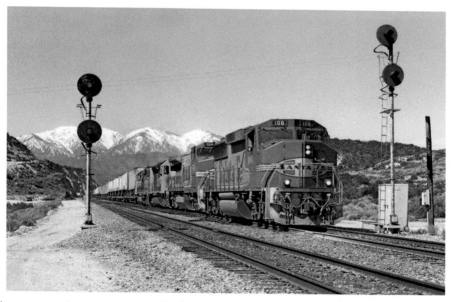

With snow on the mountains in the background, Santa Fe EMD GP60M 3,800-hp Bo-Bo diesel-electric No. 106 and GE B40-8W 4,000-hp Bo-Bo diesel-electric No. 524, both in Warbonnet livery, assist a pair of SD40-2s on an eastbound intermodal freight at Summit, Cajon Pass, California, USA. The 'Warbonnet' livery was designed for Santa Fe's 'Super Chief' train, which ran from Chicago to Los Angeles and was used from the 1930s until 1971, when the train was discontinued. It was resurrected in the late 1980s and was finally abandoned following the creation of the Burlington Northern Santa Fe Railway in 1995. 31 March 1995.

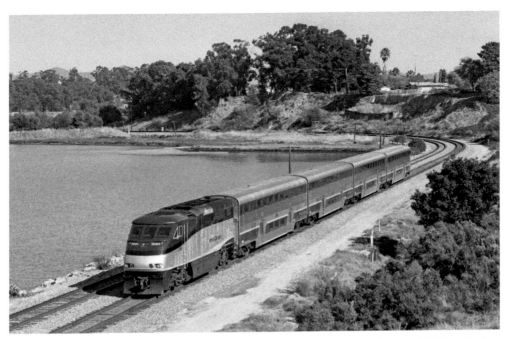

Amtrak California EMD F59PHI Bo-Bo diesel-electric No. 2005 propels the 12.40 San José to Sacramento along the Pacific coast at Pinole, California. Introduced in 1994, eighty-three of these 3,000-hp locomotives were built for passenger service in the USA. 16 October 1997.

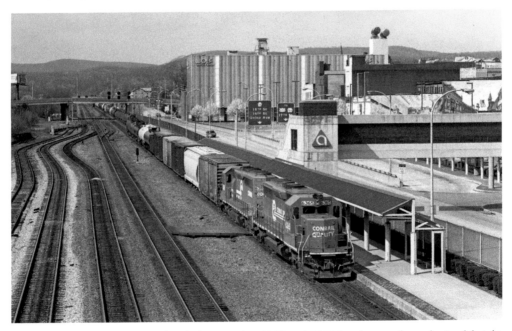

Conrail EMD SD40-2 Co-Co diesel-electrics Nos 6365 and 6385 head an eastbound mixed freight through Altoona station, Pennsylvania, USA. Conrail, the Consolidated Rail Corporation, was taken over and divided by CSX Corporation and the Norfolk Southern Railway in 1998. 28 April 1996.

Vietnam

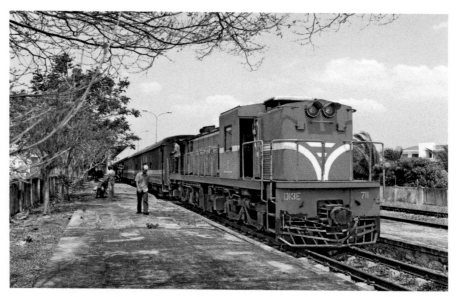

Vietnam Railways (DSVN) Co-Co diesel-electric D13E.711 stands at Phan Thiet after arriving with the 06.40 from Saigon. Twenty-five of these ALCo YDM4 locomotives, fitted with 1,350-hp engines, were supplied to Vietnam by DLW in the 1980s. They are similar to the ones used in Cambodia, Malaysia and Myanmar, but with higher cab roofs. 14 March 2019.

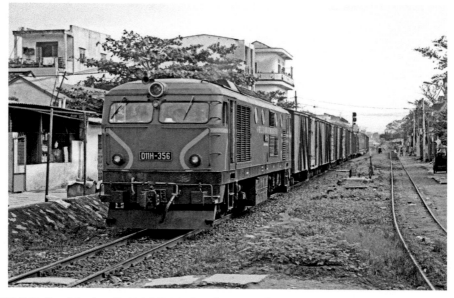

DSVN B-B diesel-hydraulic D11H.356 heads a mixed freight away from Da Nang. Between 1978 and 1980, fifty-eight 1,100-hp D11H locomotives, model LD-110-M-VN2, were built by the 23rd August Works, Romania. 3 January 2006.

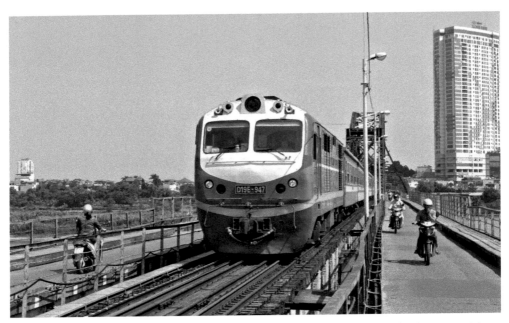

DSVN Co-Co diesel-electric D19E.947 trails at the rear of the empty stock of train LP6 from Haiphong to Long Biên, as it crosses Long Biên Bridge over the Red River hauled by D12E.655, bound for Gia Lâm. A total of eighty of these 1,950-hp D19E locomotives, in two different versions, were built by CSR Zhiyang, China, and the Gia Lâm workshops in Vietnam between 2003 and 2007. 4 November 2019.

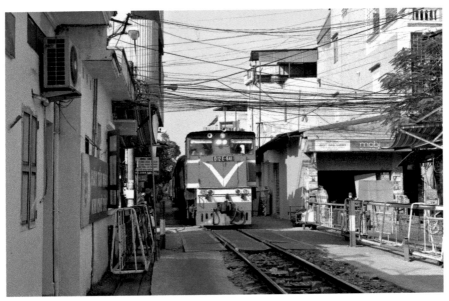

DSVN Bo-Bo diesel-electric D12E.641 nears Haiphong station with train HP1, the 06.07 Long Biên to Haiphong. Forty of these 1,200-hp locomotives, model DEV-736, were supplied to DSVN by ČKD, Prague, between 1985 and 1990. Similar locomotives were built for Cambodia. 8 November 2019.

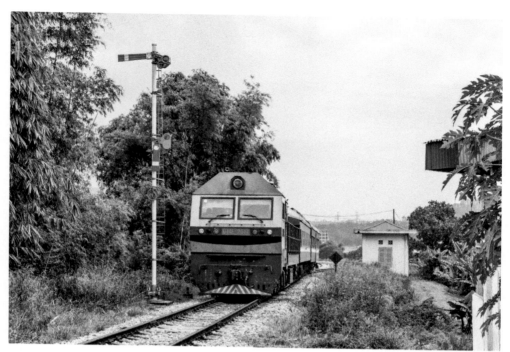

DSVN Co-Co diesel-electric D14E.2011 heads train 51502, the 13.45 Hạ Long to Yên Viên away from Hạ Long. This 1,300-hp standard gauge locomotive is one of five built for DSVN by CSR Qishuyan in 2002. 13 November 2019.

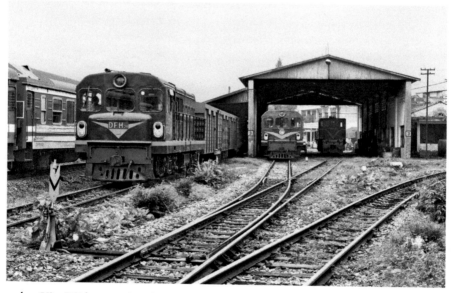

Pictured at Yên Bái locomotive depot are, from left to right, B-B diesel-hydraulic D10H.009, B-B diesel-hydraulic D10H.012, and Bo-Bo diesel-electric D12E.647. Thirty 1,000-hp D10H locomotives were purchased second-hand from China, Chinese Class DFH21, in 2006. They were built by Sifang, China, in 1977. 16 November 2019.

Zambia

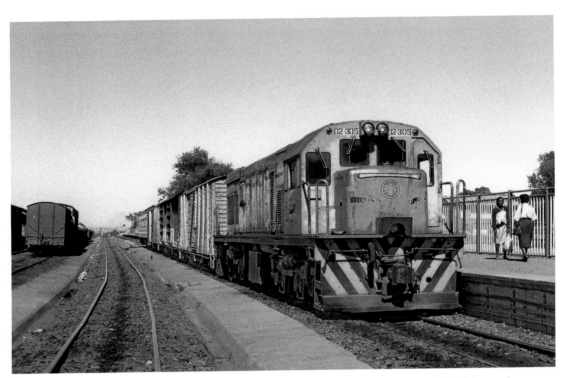

Zambia Railways (ZR) General Electric U15C Co-Co diesel-electric No. 02.305 stands at Livingstone railway station, Zambia, after arriving with a cross-border mixed train from Victoria Falls, Zimbabwe. 29 June 1996.

Zimbabwe

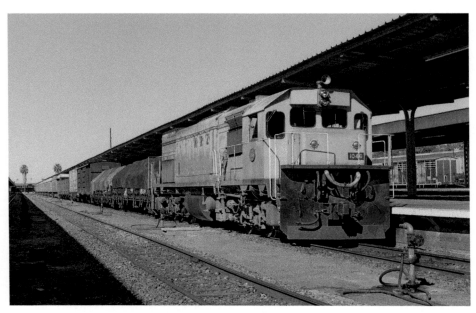

National Railways of Zimbabwe (NRZ) DE10A Class Co-Co diesel-electric No. 1046, a GM GT22LC-2, waits for departure time at Bulawayo with the 14.30 mixed train to Lobatse. Introduced in 1982, twenty-six of these locomotives were built by EMD and GMD for NRZ. 1 July 1996.

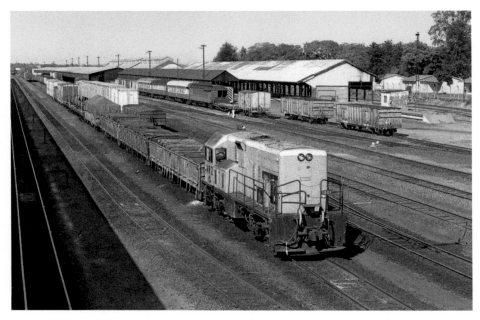

NRZ DE9 Bo-Bo diesel-electric No. 1901, a GE U10B, shunts a freight train at Bulawayo station. Twenty of these 900-hp locomotives were built by Babcock & Wilcox for NRZ. 1 July 1996.

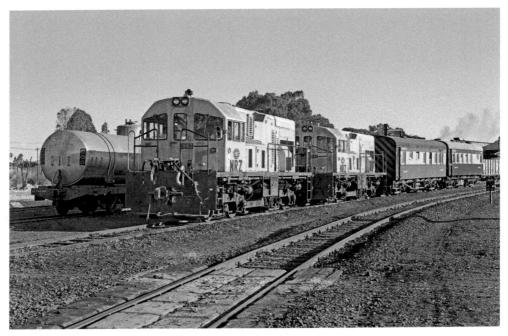

NRZ Bo-Bo diesel-electrics Nos 1963 and 1961 shunt coaching stock at Bulawayo steam shed. Forty-four of these GE U11B locomotives were built by Babcock & Wilcox for NRZ. They are NRZ Class DE9A. 23 June 1996.

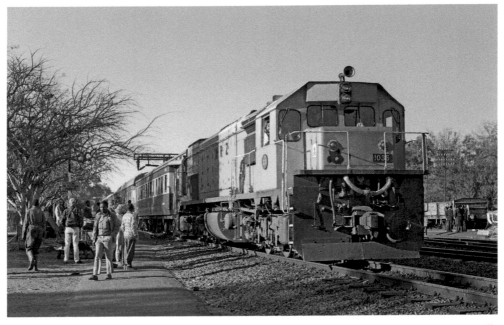

NRZ DE10 Class Co-Co diesel-electric No. 1035, an EMD GT22LC-2, stands at Victoria Falls station after arriving with a special train from Bulawayo. Thirty-five of these locomotives were built for NRZ in 1981 and 1982. 28 June 1996.